Lisa Smedman

FROM BONESHAKERS TO CHOPPERS

The Rip-Roaring History of Motorcycles

 annick press
toronto + new york + vancouver

Annick Press Ltd.

We acknowledge the support of the Canada Council for the Arts, the Ontario Arts Council, the Government of Canada through the Book Publishing Industry Development Program (BPIDP) and the Ontario Book Publishing Tax Credit (OBPTC) for our publishing activities.

Edited by Barbara Pulling and Antonia Banyard
Copy edited by Derek Fairbridge
Proofread by Melissa Edwards
Photo research by Lisa Smedman and Antonia Banyard
Cover and interior design by Irvin Cheung and Chris Freeman/iCheung Design
Front cover photo: Irvin Cheung
Back cover photos: (top) Photo courtesy Harley-Davidson USA;
(bottom) Photo by David "Foto" Avila. Photos courtesy Starboyz.

Cataloguing in Publication
Smedman, Lisa
    From boneshakers to choppers : the rip-roaring history of motorcycles / by Lisa Smedman.

Includes bibliographical references and index.
ISBN-13: 978-1-55451-016-0 (bound)
ISBN-10: 1-55451-016-3 (bound)
ISBN-13: 978-1-55451-015-3 (pbk.)
ISBN-10: 1-55451-015-5 (pbk.)

    1. Motorcycles—History—Juvenile literature. I. Title.
TL440.15.S64 2007   j629.227'5   C2006-904308-6

Printed and bound in China

Published in the U.S.A. by
Annick Press (U.S.) Ltd.

Distributed in Canada by
Firefly Books Ltd.
66 Leek Crescent
Richmond Hill, ON
L4B 1H1

Distributed in the U.S.A. by
Firefly Books (U.S.) Inc.
P.O. Box 1338
Ellicott Station
Buffalo, NY 14205

Visit our website at **www.annickpress.com**

Today, riders of all ages enjoy motorbikes of all sizes.

THE PASSION FOR MOTORCYCLES

Ever since the 1800s, when the first "motor bicycle" roared onto the scene, motorcycles have captured our imagination like no other machine. We still celebrate them in movies, books, magazines, comic books, design exhibitions and in fashion. Whether you admire them from a distance, are a first-time rider, or a long-time devotee, you're part of a huge, diverse community of fans. What is it about the motorcycle that inspires such passion?

To begin, the motorcycle gives its rider a sense of freedom—there's nothing between you and the outside world. You feel the wind in your face, the hot sun on your back, or the cold sting of rain. And there's no denying that many enjoy the sheer speed, and with it, the scent of danger. Not only can riding a motorbike be an exhilarating experience, it's also affordable—most models are cheaper than cars and less costly to run. Riders also identify with their bikes—their sleekness, their stylish design, their signature paint job. Quite simply, a motorcycle becomes an extension of the rider's identity.

So how did this infatuation begin?

The motorcycle's origin was modest. The first models were not much more than motorized bicycles—clunky in design, rough to ride, messy, and temperamental. Enthusiasts kept tinkering away, trying to improve the performance of their bikes and fulfill their dream of freedom on the road. From the start, inventors raced their one-of-a kind prototypes, in some cases riding them so fast the machines nearly tore to pieces.

By the early 1900s inventors built factories and started mass producing their designs. William Harley, along with his friends Arthur and Walter Davidson, were among those first innovators. As soon as the average person could buy a ready-made motorbike, customers clamored for the new machines.

Before long, motorbikes were racing along muddy roads in World War I, delivering messages to the front lines and carrying the wounded back to medical stations. After the war, new speed records were set and broken as eager designers continued to improve upon the basic styling. During the Great Depression,

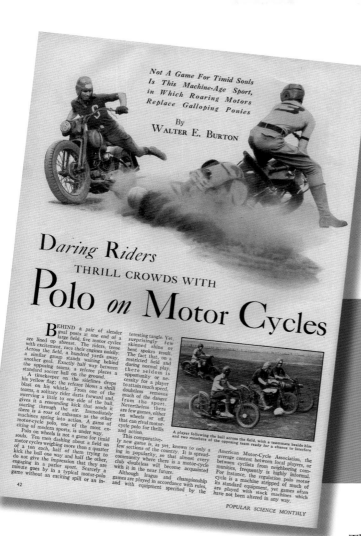

Not A Game For Timid Souls Is This Machine-Age Sport, in Which Roaring Motors Replace Galloping Ponies

By
WALTER E. BURTON

Daring Riders
THRILL CROWDS WITH
Polo on Motor Cycles

BEHIND a pair of slender goal posts at one end of a large field, five motor cycles are lined up abreast. The riders, tense with excitement, race their engines noisily. Across the field, a hundred yards away, a similar group stands waiting behind another goal. Exactly half way between the opposing teams, a referee places a standard soccer ball on the ground.

A timekeeper on the sidelines drops his yellow flag; the referee blows a shrill blast on his whistle. From one of the teams, a solitary rider darts forward and, swerving a little to one side of the ball, gives it a resounding kick that sends it soaring through the air. Immediately there is a roar of exhausts as the other machines spring into action. A game of motor-cycle polo, one of the most exciting of modern sports, is under way.

Polo on wheels is not a game for timid souls. Ten men dashing about a field on motor cycles weighing more than a quarter of a ton each, half of them trying to kick the ball one way and half the other, do not give the impression that they are engaging in a parlor sport. Scarcely a minute goes by in a typical motor-polo game without an exciting spill or an in-

teresting tangle. Yet, surprisingly few skinned shins or bent spokes result. The fact that, on a restricted field and during normal play, there seldom is opportunity or necessity for a player to attain much speed, doubtless removes much of the danger from the sport. Nevertheless there are few games, either on wheels or off, that can rival motor-cycle polo for thrills and action.

This comparatively new game is, as yet, known to only a few sections of the country. It is spreading in popularity, so that almost every community where there is a motor-cycle club doubtless will become acquainted with it in the near future.

Although league and championship games are played in accordance with rules, and with equipment specified by the

American Motor-Cycle Association, the average contest between local players, or between cyclists from neighboring communities, frequently is highly informal. For instance, the regulation polo motor cycle is a machine stripped of much of its standard equipment, yet games often are played with stock machines which have not been altered in any way.

A player following the ball across the field, with a teammate beside him and two members of the opposing team ready for a chance to interfere

42

POPULAR SCIENCE MONTHLY

Motorcycle polo required top-notch riding skills and the willingness to take a few falls. "Not a game for timid souls," this magazine article warned. "Scarcely a minute goes by...without an exciting spill or an interesting tangle." The game was played with two five-rider teams and a soccer ball.

though, sales grew sluggish. The new concept of the assembly line-made cars less expensive, so the motorbike was no longer a contender as the family vehicle. Manufacturers struggled. But as World War II loomed, the motorcycle hit the battlefield once more. Some were fitted with treads that made them look like miniature tanks, while folding motorcycles were parachuted to agents behind enemy lines.

The war ended, and veterans returned home, but many weren't ready to fit into a conventional lifestyle. The motorcycle found a new niche as a vehicle for the adventurous and the rebellious. They appealed to this new kind of "bad boy" and were soon their machine of choice. Before long, "outlaw" motorcycle clubs like the Hells Angels clashed with police, and the "biker" was born. For many, riding a motorcycle was an act of defiance and

a way to assert personal freedom. A new sub-culture evolved.

With the arrival of Japanese bikes in the 1960s, a completely different brand of rider emerged—one much less subversive, but equally in love with the freedom of the motorcycle. If there was ever any doubt about the broad appeal of the motorcycle, it quickly evaporated.

Thanks to the motorcycle and the imagination of its riders, daredevil acts emerged, adventurers undertook grueling round-the-world tours, and oddly-themed races were staged, together with those of a more conventional nature, such as drag races. Clubs of all descriptions formed, while increasingly sleek designs and steadily improving engines responded to consumer demand.

Freedom and adventure, combined with an exhaust-whiff of danger, are part of the irresistible allure of the motorcycle. From the time the first motor was mounted on a bicycle to the choppers of today, these two-wheeled wonders have had a remarkable history.

For many people, like this couple in Cambodia, a motorbike is the best way to get around.

THE FIRST "MOTOR BICYCLES"

Today's motorcycle is a meticulously designed machine of streamlined aluminum alloy and steel. Trimmed with gleaming chrome and painted in brilliant colors, it is equipped with an engine capable of launching it from zero to 100 kilometers (60 miles) per hour in three seconds flat.

The motorcycle didn't start out this way. The first gas-engine motorcycle, built by German engineer Gottlieb Daimler in 1885, was made almost entirely of wood and had a top speed of only about 10 kilometers (six miles) per hour.

Gottlieb Daimler built his *einspur* in 1885 to test out an experimental gasoline engine. The machine was made almost entirely out of wood. This photo is of a reproduction that was built for the National Motorcycle Museum in Iowa—the original *einspur* was destroyed in a fire around 1903.

Even though the earliest motorcycles were slower than a galloping horse, inventors saw their potential. During the 1800s, everything from factories to household appliances became mechanized. Everyday life sped up as machines allowed people to cram more work into less time. Walking, like any other non-mechanized activity, was seen as inefficient. The inventors of the first motorcycles knew that, one day, their vehicles would, like the cars that were evolving at the same time, take people farther and faster than they had ever gone before.

If you were to take a modern bicycle and bolt onto it one of the battery-powered electric motors you can find in bike stores today, you'd have a hard time getting anyone to agree that the end result was a "motorcycle." Yet that's exactly what the first motorcycles were: motorized bicycles. In fact, the very year after the first bicycle was invented, someone thought of putting a motor on it.

That first bicycle was built in 1817 by German inventor Baron Karl Drais von Sauerbronn. His *laufmaschine* ("walking machine") was a wooden contraption with two wheels but no pedals. It was intended to make walking easier by supporting part of the rider's weight. The rider straddled a bench-like seat and pushed himself along with his feet, using handlebars to steer. Von Sauerbronn used it for leisurely strolls around public gardens.

POWERED BY STEAM

In 1884, in the tiny stagecoach town of Phoenix, Arizona, a young steam engineer and champion bicycle racer named Lucius Copeland took a big-wheeled "penny-farthing" bike and mounted a steam engine on it. He took a "header" on his first ride and wound up in hospital with a

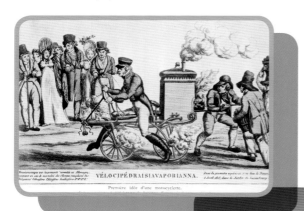

VÉLOCIPÉDRAISIAVAPORIANNA.

Première idée d'une motocyclette.

Even before the first pedal-driven bicycle was invented, people dreamed of creating a two-wheeled motorized vehicle. The *Velocipedraisia Vaporianna* in this drawing from 1818 was likely just an idea, and never built in real life.

concussion. But that didn't stop him. He mounted the engine on a second bike—this one a more stable machine because it had the small wheel in the front.

This time, it worked. Copeland's engine—made from scavenged components, including brass parts from musical instruments—chugged along nicely at a speed of about 25 kilometers (15 miles) per hour. It could run for about a half-hour before running out of coal and losing steam pressure.

While Copeland was experimenting with big-wheeled bicycles, other inventors were mounting steam engines on a more stable frame—the "safety bicycle." Inventors in France and Germany also experimented with steam-powered motorcycles, but none of these proved very practical. Steam engines were hot, heavy, and spewed spark-filled exhaust. What's more, the bike had to be stopped every dozen kilometers so the firebox could be stoked with more coal.

THE ENGINE THAT COULD

These days, aside from the occasional electric automobile or scooter, the vast majority of vehicles on the road contain an internal combustion engine. Unlike steam engines, these engines are self-contained. The pistons are inside the engine itself and are driven by a fuel-air mixture that ignites and explosively expands.

An American named Samuel Morey patented the first of these "explosion engines" in 1826, but it wasn't until the 1870s that Nikolaus Otto of Germany perfected what came to be known as

Bicycle racer Lucius Copeland attached a steam engine to this big-wheeled Star bicycle in 1884. He held demonstrations in roller skating rinks, but no one bought any of his machines. Copeland was too far ahead of his time—and by the time people were ready for his invention, gasoline had become the fuel of choice and steam engines were becoming obsolete.

The Fast Foot

The first pedal-driven bicycle was invented by Scottish blacksmith Kirkpatrick Macmillan in the late 1830s. His pedals used a crank arrangement—the pedals were suspended from the front of the frame and drove the rear wheel by means of rods—but it wasn't long until bike makers began attaching pedals directly to the front wheel, like those on a child's tricycle. The *velocipede* ("fast foot") was born. Since one rotation of the pedals equaled one rotation of the wheel, the larger the wheel, the faster the *velocipede* would go. The bike makers increased the size of the front wheel until it was chest-high.

These bicycles were called "penny farthings" because their wheels reminded people of the English coins of the day: a large penny and a small farthing. Unstable and difficult to climb onto, they were intended for indoor "riding academies," but people insisted on riding them down public streets. They had no suspension, so the cyclist could feel every bump. Back then, roads weren't paved with smooth asphalt but with uneven cobblestones. A bicycle ride was so rough that people called their bikes "boneshakers." If the front wheel hit a pothole, the rider might be catapulted off.

The "safety bicycle" of the late 1870s helped solve this problem. It had two equal-sized wheels, a seat positioned at the midpoint of a diamond-shaped frame, and pedals that drove the rear wheel by means of a chain.

The only way to make a "penny farthing" faster was to increase the size of the front wheel. Some wheels were almost as tall as the riders.

the "four-stroke engine." Then two of Otto's employees, Gottlieb Daimler and Wilhelm Maybach, struck out on their own and developed the engine further. For fuel, Daimler bought a bottle of a common hair-lice remedy called "petroleum spirit"—what we know today as petrol or gasoline. The engine was too small to power a heavy, four-wheeled carriage, so Daimler mounted it on a homemade, two-wheeled vehicle instead and called it an *einspur* (meaning "single track" in German).

Daimler never rode the *einspur* himself; he got his son Paul to test ride it. Paul must have enjoyed the ride because he took the *einspur* for a spin several times more, riding back and forth to a nearby town. Daimler hadn't realized he'd created something that was so much fun. But fun was what bicycles were all about in the late 1800s.

"HEADER"

Falling headfirst over the front of a motorcycle and hitting the ground. The saying originated with bicycle riders.

Before the bicycle was invented, people had to walk wherever they were going, unless they could afford the cost of a train ticket or had their own horse and carriage. Bicycles enabled people to easily escape towns and cities to see the countryside. For the first time, it was possible to travel to another town and back in a single day at no cost. Bicycles were cheaper than horses, since they didn't need to be fed

STOP After inventing the *einspur,* the first gasoline-powered motorcycle, Gottlieb Daimler turned to his main goal—building an automobile. He abandoned the *einspur* and went on to found the Daimler Motor Company, maker of the Mercedes.

Is It a Car? Is It a Motorcycle?

Many of the early motorcycle inventors switched back and forth between two-wheeled, three-wheeled and four-wheeled designs as they kept changing their minds about how many people their vehicles should transport. Eventually, a dividing line became clear. A car was a vehicle with three or four wheels, some sort of enclosed body in which the driver and passengers sat, and a steering wheel. A motorcycle had two wheels, handlebars, and a saddle the driver straddled. At most, it had room for one passenger, who sat behind the driver.

or stabled. The average person could afford one. Young men showed off their athletic prowess by riding them around town, and by the late 1860s were competing in organized races on the roads between towns in Europe.

Bicycle dealerships began appearing everywhere in Europe and North America; some even hired trick riders to perform stunts as a way of attracting customers. Special academies sprang up to teach people how to ride. Office buildings installed bike racks in their lobbies. Cities built bike lanes in an effort to get cyclists to stop riding on sidewalks and imposed speed limits to combat collisions between bicycles and horse-drawn vehicles at intersections.

The first motorized bicycles competed directly with regular bicycles for customers. People were drawn to the "motor cycles"

The German-made *Gebirgs* ("Mountain") *Cyklonette* had the front end of a motorcycle and a back seat with room enough for two.

Neuestes Zweicilinder-Modell!

Gebirgs-Cyklonette

CYKLON · Maschinenfabrik m. b. H. Alt-Boxhagen 18 a. BERLIN O.

because they could go faster and further—and with less physical effort. As one ad would boast in the early 1900s, the rider of a motorized bicycle "no longer pushes, pants, and perspires."

These early motorcycles, however, were still very much in the prototype stage. While it only seems natural today that a motorcycle's engine should be mounted low on the frame, between the two wheels for maximum stability, this wasn't obvious, back in the late 1800s. Early designers experimented with a number of different engine positions: beside the rear wheel, above the front wheel (which made steering difficult), and at various places on the frame. One Italian inventor even put the engine on a trailer behind the bike, with its own wheel.

BRING ON THE BIKES

In 1895 American inventor Edward Joel Pennington demonstrated his prototype motorcycle in Milwaukee. His promotional material included a drawing of it leaping over a river—something it probably wasn't capable of doing. Although Pennington was known for grandiose plans—he also claimed to be working on high-speed monorails, electric trains powered by "earth currents," and a motorized baby buggy—his demonstration may have inspired two later giants of the motorcycle industry. The teenaged

DIED IN THE SADDLE.

—Sylvester H. Roper Was Riding a Steam-Propelled Bicycle.

Had Made Fast Time on Charles River Park When He Suddenly Fell—Had Shut Off the Steam as If on Premonition of the End.

In 1896 Sylvester Roper became the first person in history to die while riding a motorcycle. Roper had taken his motorcycle to a track to see how fast it could go. He completed three laps in good time, but then wiped out after his front wheel began to wobble. Doctors later decided the 73-year-old had suffered a heart attack during the crash.

Edward Joel Pennington tried to attract investors with a demonstration of his prototype "motor-driven bicycle" in Milwaukee in 1895. Though this illustration would have been inspiring to early riders, it likely exaggerates the machine's capabilities.

William S. Harley and Arthur Davidson were living in Milwaukee that year and may have seen him.

Less than a decade later they—and hundreds of other young inventors and entrepreneurs just like them around the world—would set up the first motorcycle factories. The days of turning out one-of-a-kind prototypes were about to end. The turn of the century would see the birth of the mass-produced, brand-name motorcycle.

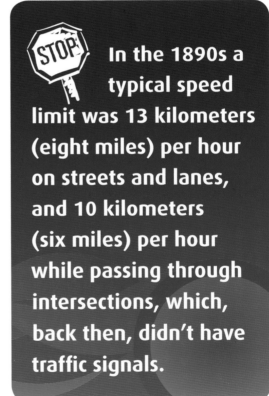

STOP **In the 1890s a typical speed limit was 13 kilometers (eight miles) per hour on streets and lanes, and 10 kilometers (six miles) per hour while passing through intersections, which, back then, didn't have traffic signals.**

2 ADVENTURE ON TWO WHEELS

In 1900, 20-year-old F.J. Wiggert purchased a two-seated tandem bicycle and cut off what he didn't need with a hacksaw. He then mounted a homemade engine onto what remained of the heavy-duty frame, hopped on, and took his newly invented version of a motorcycle out for a spin around his hometown of La Crosse, Wisconsin.

Today it would look strange to ride a motorcycle in a suit, coat, and hat, but in the 1910s it was quite normal. While motorcyclists could buy specialized motorcycle gear, many preferred to ride in their usual, day-to-day, clothes.

"Everywhere he went the people looked at him in amazement," the local paper would recall 18 years later. In La Crosse, as in most towns in those days, contraptions such as Wiggert's motorcycle were an oddity—something only an adventurous and "mechanically minded youth" would ride.

Although the first motorcycle brand names like Harley-Davidson, Triumph, BSA and Indian had started to appear by the early 1900s, most of these companies were producing prototypes that weren't even close to being perfected. Luckily, curious inventors around the world turned their imaginations to ironing out the many design flaws of early motorcycles.

Motorcycles of the day were temperamental. Any number of things could go wrong—and frequently did. Chains snapped and had to be repaired with spare links. A wheel that hit a rock or log would need to be re-spoked. Inner tubes frequently blew. Since shops that carried replacement tubes were few and far between, riders had to learn how to patch them themselves. Without tools, spare parts, and a basic knowledge of repairs, a motorcycle rider wasn't going far.

Even finding gasoline could be an adventure. Gas stations only existed in big cities. In smaller towns, tins of gasoline were sold in general stores, right beside

Motorcycles were once sold in bicycle shops, and manufacturers knew that a boy who rode a bicycle today might grow up to ride a motorcycle tomorrow. In 1913 the Indian motorcycle company encouraged this idea by releasing a pedal bicycle that had a pretend gas tank. In 1917, Harley-Davidson released its own bicycle, hoping to inspire brand loyalty in young kids.

Running Start

In the early 1900s riding a motorcycle took a lot of work. Starting the engine meant putting the bike on its stand and pedaling until the motor caught. The rider would then lurch the machine forward off the stand. Another way to start a motorcycle was to push it while running along beside it until the motor started, then leap onto the saddle.

Modern motorcycles have a clutch that disengages the motor, allowing it to continue running while the bike is stopped. But before the clutch became a standard feature, if a motorcycle came to a stop, so did its engine—and the rider had to go through the whole process of starting it again. Luckily there weren't many stop signs or traffic signals in those early days.

Another innovation that keeps things running smoothly these days is the throttle. It controls how much fuel enters the engine, and how fast the bike goes. The motorcycles of the early 1900s didn't have the simple twist-grip throttles found on modern bikes. Keeping the engine running involved working three different levers, mounted next to the gas tank. Imagine wrestling with three levers and trying to steer at the same time. On top of that, every few kilometers the rider had to stop the bike to lubricate the engine by hand.

Other early controls were equally primitive. Among the first brake systems were a metal bar that dragged on the road, and a metal "shoe" that rubbed against the top of the wheel, slowing it down.

Design improvements came swiftly as the first motorcycle factories sprang up across Europe and North America. By the 1910s, most motorcycles no longer had pedals. They had clutches, kick starts, and twist-grip throttles mounted on the handlebars. A few even had electric starters—although the poor batteries of the day made these unreliable.

the bolts of cloth and cans of food. Once it got dark, riding got even more challenging. The only illumination came from gas flame lamps or primitive battery-powered headlamps, neither of which did much to light up the road ahead. Riding in the country—especially on the rough dirt roads of North America, which was still mostly wilderness in the early 1900s—was something only the adventurous attempted. But this just made motorcycles that much more appealing to riders. For them, these challenges were part of the thrill.

Motorcycles weren't just exciting to ride. They were fun to read about, too. When publisher Edward Stratemeyer was looking for a machine for his fictional hero-inventor Tom Swift to get around on, he chose the motorcycle. *Tom Swift and his Motor-Cycle*, published in 1910, kick-started the series. Tom's motorcycle has its drawbacks—it throws up dust onto his clothes, crashes when its wheel hits a rock, and breaks a chain. But with a wrench, pliers, and a screwdriver, Tom makes it good as new. Better than new, in fact. The young inventor—said to have been inspired by a real-life motorcycle designer—changes a sprocket and adds a bigger gas tank, and the bike goes faster.

Tom Swift wasn't the only adventure-book hero to get around on a motorcycle.

The Motorcycle Chums series by Andrew Carey Lincoln featured four teenage boys who tackle everything from the rugged wilderness of Yellowstone Park to the Santa Fe Trail. Along the way, they have "thrilling adventures" with moonshiners, poachers, and "nomadic Apaches." A similar series, Big Five Motorcycle Boys by Ralph Marlow, had a group of

People have complained about the noise from motorcycles since the machines were first invented. This cartoon from the 1900s contrasts the gentleman rider with the "muffler fiend" who leaves his exhaust cutout open.

Problem—Which of These Two Individuals Is Doing the Most to Advance the Welfare of the Sport?

Cops on Bikes

It's difficult to pin down which police force was the first to trade in its bicycles for motorcycles, but one early contender is a unit in Yonkers, New York, which purchased an Indian in 1906. Even though speed limits were exceedingly low by today's standards, they were tough to enforce. Even horse-drawn buggies could easily lose a bicycle-mounted patrolman. Keeping up on a one-speed bike was hard work. The Indian purchased by the Yonkers Police Department was capable of today's city street speed limits, and it didn't have to slow down to take a corner like a four-wheeled vehicle did. Best of all, it had a revolutionary device called a speedometer that gave police the evidence they needed to get a speeding conviction in court.

Lieutenant Jerome F. Linehan shows off the second motorcycle purchased by the Yonkers Police Department.

motorcyclists thwarting bank robbers and other criminals. In the final three books, published at the beginning of World War I, the heroes ride with the troops at the front line.

Even the Boy Scouts mounted up. In the 1912 book *Boy Scouts on Motorcycles or With the Flying Squadron*, an intrepid group of Scouts use their motorcycles to carry out work on behalf of the U.S. Secret Service in China.

BAD PRESS

Not everyone was enthusiastic about motorcycles. Wiggert recalled that his family was "continually discouraging him." He could have taken out a patent on his motorcycle and developed it further—and later he wished he'd done just that. But after a motorcycle accident that injured his leg, Wiggert never rode again. His family must have been relieved because, even in the early 1900s, motorcyclists were starting to get bad press.

By the 1910s, some motorcycles had "exhaust cutouts"—flaps in the exhaust pipe that could be opened to allow exhaust to bypass the muffler. This increased the engine's horsepower. The cutouts were intended for use on country roads, where the extra noise wouldn't annoy anyone, but some riders used them all the time. Compared with the "clip-clop" of a horse and buggy, the roar of an unmuffled engine would have been deafening.

As if that weren't bad enough, when the motorcycle rider finally got off his noisy machine, he was a mess. On a hot day, dirt roads covered his clothes with dust. On a rainy day, he'd arrive splattered in mud. As well, his pants would be covered in oil. Early motorcycle engines had "total loss" lubricating systems, which means the oil wasn't re-circulated back into the engine, so instead it dripped out of the bottom of the bike and flew back onto the rider's legs.

STOP To protect their pants, riders wound puttees (strips of cloth) around their lower legs, or strapped on stiff leather or canvas gaiters like those worn by soldiers.

It wasn't long, however, before clothing companies began producing riding gear. One 1912 ad for "motorcycle suits" and leggings reminded riders that "today, 'gentlemen' are riding and unless you want to be classed otherwise, consider your appearance."

Heat Over Headgear

The first helmets were soft leather caps that buckled under the chin. They were designed for comfort rather than safety, and were intended to keep dust out of the hair and the wind out of a rider's ears. Though the caps provided some protection against scrapes, they did little to protect against the more severe effects of a crash, such as a fractured skull or brain injury.

Cork-lined helmets with a stiff outer shell (known as "pudding basins") were worn by racers as early as the 1920s, but it wasn't until the late 1950s that the modern motorcycle helmet was created.

The world's first mandatory helmet law was introduced in Australia in 1961; similar laws would eventually follow in other countries. In the U.S., however, bikers fought back against what they saw as an attack on their personal freedom. They formed ABATE (A Brotherhood Against Totalitarian Enactments) and held "helmet roasts." The controversy over whether wearing helmets should be mandatory continues to this day.

Hogs vs. Indians

You'll never wear out the Indian Scout
Or its brother, the Indian Chief
They're built like rocks to take hard knocks
It's the Harleys that cause the grief

Ask the average North American to name a brand of motorcycle, and chances are he or she will say "Harley."

Yet even though Harley-Davidson is known around the world today, it was just another of the dozens of motorcycle companies that sprang up in North America during the first two decades of the 1900s. Customers shopping for a motorcycle could choose from a number of equally well-known brands, including Pope, Merkel, Ace, Thor—and Indian, the company that would go on to become Harley-Davidson's chief rival for decades.

When it got its start, the Harley-Davidson "company" consisted of three guys in their early 20s tinkering with motors in a backyard shed in Milwaukee, Wisconsin. In 1901, William Harley began sketching out plans for a "bicycle motor." In 1903, with the help of brothers Arthur and Walter Davidson (whose family provided the shed), he mounted the seven-cubic-inch (115cc) motor he'd designed on a bicycle.

By the spring of 1905, Harley-Davidson was selling its motorcycles in dealerships.

Meanwhile, in Springfield, Massachusetts, engine designer Carl Oskar Hedstrom and bicycle maker George M. Hendee were busy drawing up designs of their own. In 1901 they built their first machine—which they called "Indian," a name they believed captured the "American pioneering tradition." That first "motocycle," as Hendee Manufacturing insisted on spelling it, was a motorized pacer bicycle, intended to set the pace for bicycle racers as they trained.

It wasn't long before the two American companies were in a neck-and-neck race for customers.

Both Harley-Davidson and Indian were establishing themselves as brand names in the early 1900s, just as bicycle manufacturers had done in the late 1800s. Each company strove to convince customers that it built the best machine. One way to do this was to enter their machines in speed and endurance contests.

In 1908, Walter Davidson won the two-day National Endurance and Reliability Contest in New York state. Despite the fact that two other Harley-Davidson riders failed to complete the 560-kilometer (350-mile) event, motorcycle magazines focused on the fact that the Indian riders hadn't won. Three years later, however, Indian machines placed first, second, and third in the 1911 Isle of Man

Tourist Trophy races in the United Kingdom. The company was quick to exploit the win. The next year, it released two-speed "Tourist Trophy" models. These boosted sales, and Indians outsold Harley-Davidsons by nearly two to one. Indian (then known as Hendee Manufacturing) produced more motorcycles than any other manufacturer in the world.

Most of the dozens of North American motorcycle manufacturers that sprang up in the early 1900s didn't survive. Only one would come close to Harley-Davidson or Indian in size. In the 1920s, Excelsior was one of the "big three" motorcycle manufacturers. It folded, however, in 1931. By then, only Harley-Davidson and Indian remained.

Indian was a victim of bad decisions, such as switching to smaller bikes that were intended to compete with the lightweight motorcycles the British were producing. The company did this at a time when Americans wanted big, heavy-duty motorcycles. Indian had kept going during World War II thanks to orders from the military, but the company just couldn't survive in the civilian market.

When Indian closed its doors in 1953, Harley-Davidson became the sole surviving North American motorcycle manufacturer until the 1990s, when several companies merged and Indians rode the streets again. That same decade, the Polaris snowmobile company introduced the American-built Victory motorcycle.

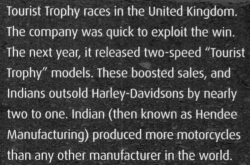

Walter Davidson poses with the Harley-Davidson motorcycle he rode to victory in the 1908 National Endurance and Reliability Contest.

FUN, FUN, FUN

Regardless of what "gentlemen" thought, riding a motorcycle was a popular "sport" in the early 1900s. That was when the first motorcycle clubs formed and members got together to ride their machines out into the country, just as bicycle clubs had done the decade before.

For their part, motorcycle manufacturers were intent on proving that, respectable or not, motorcycles were useful. Ads from the early 1900s urged farmers to buy motorcycles, calling them the perfect vehicle for a quick trip into town. Instead of wasting time hitching a horse to a wagon, a farmer could just hop on his motorcycle and go. And country doctors could use them to make house calls. To attract buyers from the city, ads promised that a motorcycle could help the working man escape the noise and smoke of the city and enjoy the countryside.

Manufacturers realized that a motorcycle was more than just a practical machine. Owning one also meant freedom. As Indian motorcycle ads from the 1910s put it, the motorcycle could deliver things an automobile couldn't: "No box of glass and wood for him...he wants to feel the sun on his back, the breeze in his hair... to venture into places no [automobile] motorist can go."

In the decades to come, that sense of adventure and freedom would be pushed to its limit.

Early ads tried to attract urban workers by contrasting the freedom of motorcycles with the tedium of slow, overcrowded street cars.

"Goodbye, Strap-Hangers"

③ PUSHING THE LIMITS

In September 2004, a Minnesota State Patrol officer spotted two motorcyclists racing along a highway. Taking out his stopwatch, he clocked the motorcycle in the lead at 350 kilometers (205 miles) per hour. The 20-year-old rider was later charged with exceeding the speed limit, driving without a motorcycle license, and reckless driving. It was, reported *USA Today*, quite possibly the fastest speed ever recorded on a speeding ticket on a U.S. highway.

Glenn Curtiss became the "fastest man in the world" in 1907. He raced his machine at speeds four times that of other motorbikes of the era. Curtiss may have been the inspiration for Tom Swift, the fictional inventor featured in a popular series of adventure novels.

Modern "superbikes" can reach speeds above 400 kilometers (250 miles) per hour. Even though these speeds are illegal—except on roads like Germany's autobahn freeways—manufacturers know that speed sells. The adrenaline rush that comes from riding a motorcycle at exceedingly high speeds isn't a modern phenomenon. As far back as the first decade of the 1900s, people were trying to see just how fast a motorcycle could go.

The earliest motorcycles weren't fast by today's standards, though. At the turn of the 20th century the average motorcycle didn't go much faster than 40 kilometers (25 miles) per hour. That's what made it so amazing when American inventor Glenn Curtiss broke the 100-miles-per-hour (160-kmph) mark in January of 1907.

The motorcycle Curtiss built had a massive V-8 engine, much larger than the two-cylinder engines commonly used to power motorcycles at the time. Afraid that it might tear from the frame, Curtiss began his run by being towed. Once he hit 65 kilometers (40 miles) per hour he started the engine and opened up the throttle. Although he was clocked by stopwatches as covering a mile in the fastest time ever, the record wasn't officially recognized because Curtiss couldn't perform a second

A number of motorcycle companies organized factory racing teams. These professional racers rode bikes designed for speed and they were paid much more than what they could earn at regular jobs. This is the Harley-Davidson "Wrecking Crew" of 1914.

run. His motorcycle's universal joint had broken and the frame had started to buckle. Even so, his unofficial record stood for 23 years.

ROAD RACING

Almost as soon as motorcycles were invented, riders started competing against one another to see who could go the fastest. The first motorcycle race was held in 1894, from Paris to Rouen, France.

In Britain, however, the laws prohibited racing on public roads, and it was impossible to get permission to close the roads for a motorcycle race. So speed enthusiasts turned to the Isle of Man, a small island off the west coast of England that is part of Britain but has its own laws. The island's roads offered a challenging course of hills, sharp turns, and bridges. Held in 1907, the Isle of Man Tourist Trophy was Britain's first official motorcycle road race. Twenty-five riders set out, but only 10 finished. The winner's average speed was 59 kilometers (36 miles) per hour. In contrast, today riders whip around the Isle of Man course at more than 190 kilometers (118 miles) per hour.

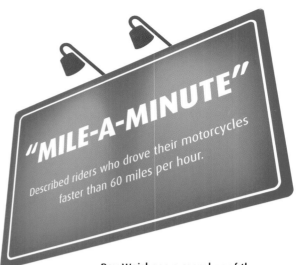

"MILE-A-MINUTE"

Described riders who drove their motorcycles faster than 60 miles per hour.

Ray Weishaar, a member of the Harley-Davidson motorcycle racing team, gives the team mascot a drink following a competition. The pig was carried on a victory lap around the track after each win, giving rise to the nickname "Hog" for Harley-Davidson motorcycles.

Dirt-track racing got its start prior to World War I, when motorcycles used horse-racing tracks. To spice up a day at the races, track owners would invite motorcycle clubs to compete before the crowds. The owners would also hire airplane pilots to give demonstration flights overhead. Sometimes a race between a motorcycle and biplane would be held, with the motorcycle speeding along the track while the biplane roared above.

"MURDERDROMES"

When motorcycles first ventured on to racetracks in Europe and North America in the late 1890s, they weren't there to race. They were only there to set the pace for the stars of the show—bicycles.

Back then, bicycle racing was hugely popular. To help cyclists increase their speed, trainers used motorized bicycles—two-seated tandem "pacers"—to lead the cyclists around the track. It wasn't long, however, before the motorcycles were being raced on their own.

Early racers wore very little protective gear—just goggles, gloves and, sometimes, a padded leather helmet.

Motorcycles were raced on dirt tracks and beaches, but races held on board tracks drew the biggest crowds. As many as 10,000 people would come out to watch the action. In this photo, taken either in the 1910s or 1920s, spectators in Tacoma lean over the rail, eagerly watching a board track race.

In those days, bicycle races were held in "velocodromes"—round or oval tracks made of two-by-four boards. Similar tracks were used for motorcycle races. Known as "motodromes," they were steeply banked—up to 62 degrees, in some cases.

By the 1910s, riders with colorful names like Paul "Dare Devil" Derkum, Erwin "Cannon Ball" Baker, Walter "Mile a Minute" Collins, and Charles "Fearless" Balke were hurtling around wooden tracks at speeds just under 160 kilometers (100 miles) per hour. On the smaller tracks, a lap took just 10 seconds. By the 1920s, racers were speeding along at up to 210 kilometers (130 miles) per hour.

The tracks were dangerous, and their owners and managers gloried in it. The Detroit Motordome featured a billboard that read "Neck and Neck with Death." Riders had minimal protection: a leather helmet and goggles. Their engines sprayed oil onto the track; those riding behind another motorcycle soon had their goggles

"MURDERDROMES"

A nickname for "motodromes" that expressed how dangerous racing on them could be.

smeared with a film of oil. Between races, the oil had to be scrubbed from the track with a lye solution.

To give the wheels traction, the track was built of boards that were rough cut (they weren't sanded smooth). When a rider lost control and fell, he could skid for 60 meters (200 feet) or more. Glen "Slivers" Boyd earned his nickname in 1912 after his rear tire blew during a race, throwing him into a slide. It took doctors two weeks to remove more than 200 wooden splinters from his body.

The thrill of board racing started to pall in 1912, after a horrendous accident at a track in New Jersey took the lives of two riders and six spectators. Eddie Hasha lost control of his bike, which skidded along the rail that separated spectators from the track, killing four young boys. The bike then slammed into a post and Hasha flew into the grandstand, fatally injuring both himself and a spectator. His bike, meanwhile, fell back onto the track, slamming into racer Johnny Albright, who skidded for some distance with Hasha's motorcycle entangled in his own. During the tumble, the rear wheel flew off Hasha's bike, fatally injuring yet another spectator standing on the infield. Albright smashed his skull, fractured a leg and dislocated a shoulder. He wound up in a coma and died five days later.

Women Go the Distance

If the early advertising was anything to go by, women weren't expected to buy motorcycles. Indian addressed its early ads to the "red-blooded, freedom-seeking man." But women were buying and riding motorcycles—and they were doing things just as dangerous and adventurous as any man.

The actress Helen Gibson, for example, performed her own motorcycle and automobile stunts for the 119-episode film series The Hazards of Helen that ran from 1914 to 1917. Originally a trick rider with a Wild-West show, Gibson was the first female action hero. In her films, she often single-handedly caught the villains.

In 1910, 18-year-old Clara Wagner won a 600-kilometer (375-mile) endurance race from Chicago to Indianapolis. When the Federation of American Motorcyclists refused to award her a trophy, her fellow racers took up a collection and bought her a gold pendant. She rode a Wagner motorcycle, built by her father. A company advertisement featured her words: "Women can ride Wagner machines as easily as men."

Other women undertook long distance rides to make the same point. In 1916, two "society girls"—sisters Adeline and Augusta Van Buren—

embarked on a coast-to-coast journey to prove that women had what it took to be military dispatch riders. They set out from Brooklyn on their matching Indian Power Plus motorcycles and arrived in Los Angeles two months later. They were arrested several times en route for their gear—men's trousers and jackets—attire that was unlawful for women to wear.

After the trip, Adeline, an English teacher, applied to become a military dispatch rider. Not surprisingly, given the attitudes of the time about women in combat, the U.S. government turned her down.

Slowly, however, manufacturers woke up to the fact that women rode. In the 1920s, Harley-Davidson ads proclaimed: "If you are an out-door girl or woman you'll glory in the 'git' and 'go' of motorcycling." But it would be many decades before a woman on a motorcycle was seen as anything other than an oddity.

Avis and Effie Hotchkiss, a mother-and-daughter team, crossed the U.S. on a Harley-Davidson in 1915. They set out from Brooklyn, NY and braved mountains, deserts and torrential rainstorms at a time when paved roads were a rarity. More than once they crashed and had to push the motorcycle to the nearest town and find a blacksmith to make replacement parts from scratch. After a two-month journey they reached San Francisco, where they dipped their wheels in the Pacific Ocean, visited the World's Fair, then turned around and rode all the way back again.

Newspapers of the day labeled board tracks "murderdromes." The New Jersey track closed down, as did several others. Board racing continued through the 1920s, however, despite numerous more injuries and deaths.

FROM OCEAN TO OCEAN

Meanwhile, other motorcycle riders were seeking fame—and adventure—by seeing just how far their machines could take them.

In the early 1900s, North America had no freeways. Most of the roads connecting cities and towns were unpaved. A heavy rainstorm could wash out bridges or fill a road with deep, wheel-clinging mud. Trees toppled by windstorms could block roads. And, back then, there weren't as many towns. When a motorcycle broke down, riders who couldn't fix their own bikes

were faced with a long and difficult walk to the nearest town.

To the adventurous, these hazards were an irresistible challenge.

Erwin "Cannon Ball" Baker, a stunt rider, sometimes raced his motorcycle against trains. In 1914 he set a record by crossing the U.S. west to east in 11 days, 12 hours and 10 minutes. This photo shows him with a Neracar he used on a 1920s run from New York to Los Angeles.

The "world's toughest motorcycle competition" is the biannual Iron Butt Rally. It's an 11-day, 17,700-kilometer (11,000-mile) ride around the perimeter of the United States that includes both desert and mountain terrain.

Little wonder then, that the first motorized vehicle to cross the North American continent was a motorcycle. That was in 1903, and the rider was George Wyman. His sponsors, the motorcycle manufacturer California Motor Company and the magazine *Bicycle World*, offered him a $500 bonus if he completed the 6,300-kilometer (3,900-mile) trip from San Francisco to New York City in 40 days. Wyman gave it his best shot, riding along railroad tracks in places where there were no roads, but snow slowed him down. It took him 51 days to reach New York. He didn't get the bonus.

We travel a lot more these days, and it doesn't take us much time to get where we're going. A trip across a continent is a short hop in an airplane. But in the early days of motorized vehicles, almost every long-distance trip broke a record or made history. And going around the world was the most ambitious journey of all.

The first around-the-world airplane flight took place in 1924. At about the same time, motorcyclists were also circling the globe by riding on land and ferrying their bikes across the intervening oceans by ship. In 1926 two Frenchmen rode around the world, traveling east through Europe, Russia and Japan before crossing the U.S. and riding home to Paris again.

Other motorcyclists set records by riding around in circles.

Twenty-four-hour endurance races became popular in the 1920s. The idea was for a single rider to complete as many laps of a track as possible within 24 hours. In 1922, Wells Bennett managed 2,514.66 kilometers (1,562.54 miles)—close to the distance from Los Angeles to Baton Rouge—on a board track, a record that stood for 15 years. It was a grueling ride, and Bennett had to be helped off the bike at the end of it.

Long Distance Legacy

The endurance competitions that began in the 1910s left a legacy that continues today. Modern endurance runs include the Paris-Dakar Rally, which begins in France, hops the Mediterranean by boat to the deserts of Morocco, and ends in Dakar, Senegal. Only about a quarter of the riders who enter actually finish the more than 15,000-kilometer (9,300-mile) race, which can take up to three weeks to complete. Eleven motorcyclists have died attempting to complete the race since its inception in 1978. In North America, the Three Flags Run started in the 1910s as an endurance race organized by motorcycle clubs. It continues today, as the Three Flags Classic, run from Tijuana, Mexico, to Vancouver, British Columbia (or vice versa).

Modern adventurers still make round-the-world trips by motorcycle. In 2003, Sergey Sinelnik of Moscow—along with his brother, a mechanic and a cameraman—rode through Africa from north to south before continuing across the rest of the world.

4 THE MOTORCYCLE GOES TO WAR

When motorcycles came into use, military commanders instinctively knew that they would be as effective in war as horses had been. They just weren't sure, at first, how they could be used. Somebody, somewhere, probably looked at a motorcycle and imagined a motorized cavalry charge. It never happened for one simple reason. In order to use a cavalry weapon, a motorcycle rider would have needed a third hand. With a horse, it's possible to drop the reins and "steer" with your knees. But steering a motorcycle over the bumpy terrain of a battlefield requires both hands.

In World War I, motorcycles outfitted with stretchers served as makeshift ambulances.

Straight Shooters

Aside from artillery, the weapon that most dominated World War I was the machine gun. In an attempt to turn the machine gun into a mobile weapon, the British mounted Vickers machine guns onto motorcycle sidecars. These guns, however, were almost impossible to shoot accurately if the motorcycle was traveling over bumpy ground. Some gunners even shot out their motorcycle's front wheel.

There were also problems with the motorcycles themselves. Although it was called the "trusty Triumph" in ads, the British Triumph Model H used in World War I was anything but. On rough terrain, the front fork spring would snap, causing the bike's front end to collapse. Dispatch riders used to wrap a heavy leather strap around the front end to keep the bike together, just in case.

During World War I some motorcycle sidecars were equipped with machine guns and armor, but they were rarely used in battle.

Despite its unsuitability as a cavalry mount, the motorcycle was perfect for infantry scouting. The military had used bicycles for scouting since the 1870s, but they had their disadvantages. A soldier who pedaled to his destination would arrive out of breath, especially if he had to climb a hill. A motorcycle could get him there twice as fast—and not fatigued.

In 1904, British lieutenant H.G. de Watteville mused on the possible military uses for a motorcycle. It had, he noted, several advantages. First, it was two and a half times as fast as a horse over longer distances. And it could go places a horse-drawn vehicle couldn't. A motorcycle could thread its way through a column of marching soldiers and turn around quickly on a narrow road. Scouts on reconnaissance missions could conceal a motorcycle behind bushes—something they couldn't do with a horse or larger vehicle.

The lieutenant proposed that motorcycles be used to move soldiers into combat in the same manner as dragoons—soldiers who rode on horseback to the front, dismounted, and fought on foot with rifles. The lieutenant imagined up to 30 motorcyclists riding into battle with

On November 12, 1918—one day after the official end of the war—Corporal Roy Holtz rode into Germany on his sidecar-equipped Harley-Davidson motorcycle, which made him, according to the Harley-Davidson *Enthusiast* magazine, the first American on record to enter post-war Germany.

Hunting Revolutionaries on Two Wheels

The first time motorcycles were used by the United States Army was in 1916, a year before the U.S. entered World War I. Motorcycles were part of the force sent to capture a Mexican revolutionary.

That year, Pancho Villa and his "pistoleros" rode across the border into New Mexico to attack a U.S. Cavalry camp and shoot up a nearby town. The U.S. military ordered Brigadier General John "Black Jack" Pershing to capture Villa, and the hunt was on.

The force Pershing led into Mexico was a mix of the old and the new. Supplies were carried both on the backs of mules and by truck. Cavalry patrolled on horseback, while Curtiss JN-2 "Jenny" biplanes provided aerial reconnaissance. Included in the more than 10,000-man force were several motorcycles. Some worked with the 1st Aero Squadron, carrying mechanics to downed airplanes. Others had sidecars fitted with machine guns.

The expedition never did catch Villa, but it marked the first time mechanized vehicles of any kind—either two-wheeled or four-wheeled—had been used by the U.S. military in combat.

"Having a lovely war, wish you were here." This postcard commemorates the U.S. expedition into Mexico to catch the revolutionary Pancho Villa and his *pistoleros*.

Armored Truck and Motorcycle in action

rifles strapped vertically to the front forks of their bikes, and ammunition and kit strapped elsewhere onto the frame of the bike.

But World War I, which lasted from 1914 to 1918,was primarily fought in trenches, with soldiers holding the same piece of ground for months on end. A typical attack might only capture an amount of ground equal to the length of a football field, so there was little moving back and forth. Motorcycle dragoons never became a reality. Nor was the motorcycle able to do much scouting. The airplane took up that duty.

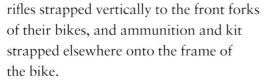

Instead, motorcycles were used to transport everything from messages, to the wounded. The one thing a motorcycle couldn't do, however, was transport a wireless radio set to the front. The radios used in World War I were fragile. The bumpy ride would have destroyed them. Instead motorcyclists carried another communications device used in that war: carrier pigeons. The birds jolted along in wicker baskets on the rider's back. Pigeons might seem a primitive way of getting messages back from the front lines, but they worked...most of the time.

Another big job for motorcycles during World War I was escort duty. A motorcyclist could ride up and down a column of supply trucks or marching soldiers, passing messages from the front of the column to the rear.

WHEELS INTO WAR

In 1939 the world went to war once again. By this time, motorcycles were easier to ride and more durable. In addition to scouting and delivering messages, in World War II, motorcycles also wound up in combat. Unlike in the "Great War," the battles of World War II ranged over vast distances.

Allied dispatch riders were trained to ride through smoke, to ride with a gas mask on, and to send their machines into a slide that would allow them to lay prone and open fire with a machine gun.

The Germans saw motorcycles as attack vehicles and organized them into battalions. Each motorcycle carried three soldiers: a driver and rifleman on the motorcycle itself, and a machine

Members of the 5th Canadian Motorcycle Regiment trained on motorcycles in Victoria, Canada during World War II. The motorcycle training wasn't needed, however—in Europe they used tanks to fight in the Italian campaign.

gunner in a sidecar. During the German blitzkrieg ("lightning war"), these machines raced ahead to flank the enemy.

The Germans also developed perhaps the strangest-looking motorcycle yet. Introduced in 1942, the *kettenkraftrad* ("chain-driven wheel," usually shortened to *kettenkrad*) was a motorcycle with tank tracks on the back that would propel it through anything: snow, mud, or sand. It had a saddle for the rider, plus a seat in back for two other soldiers. It was also capable of pulling a trailer. The *kettenkraftrad* must have been useful, since by the war's end more than 8,300 had been built.

The Allied Powers, which included the U.S., Britain, France, and other allies, came up with some strange motorcycles of their own. One was a motorcycle fitted with a snorkel-like device that, in theory, prevented ocean water from drowning the engine during beach landings. A motorcycle rising

The *kettenkraftrad* was developed by the Germans during World War II. This strange vehicle combined elements of the motorcycle and the tank.

STOP **During World War I motorcycles were used like tractors to pull small-caliber artillery, and to patrol telephone and radio lines to search for breaks in the wire.**

out of the surf would have been a strange sight, indeed, but it's doubtful this design worked very well.

The Allies also came up with machines designed to withstand the heat and dust of North Africa. Here the Axis Powers, including Italy and Nazi Germany, battled the Allies for control of such countries as Egypt, Libya, and Tunisia. After the fall of France, North Africa was the only place where the Allies were fighting the Germans and Italians in a land battle. This "Desert War" helped pull German forces away from the Eastern Front, in Russia. That's what made it so important.

MAY 11, 1916

MOTORCYCLE RIOT GUN OUTFITS SUGGESTED FOR NEW YORK POLICE

Fighting on the Home Front

The early decades of the 20th century were a time of unrest. International labor unions organized workers to demand a decent wage and a shorter workday. Entire cities in North America were shut down by general strikes that closed almost every business in town. These strikes were often brutally suppressed by the police, who arrested union organizers and threw them in jail.

In 1916 the New York Police Department proposed the use of machine gun-equipped motorcycle sidecars to put down labor "riots"—violent confrontations that had more often than not been started when police waded into a peaceful crowd with batons swinging. Thankfully, these motorcycles were never used to gun strikers down.

Armored police motorcycles did come into use during the Prohibition era, however, when the sale of alcohol was illegal and "bootleggers" sold booze on the "black market," much in the same way illegal drugs are sold today. In 1929 the New York police purchased 21 armored motorcycles and sidecars with bulletproof windshields. Six were used by the "Gunman's Squad," which targeted organized crime.

Motorcycle in a Can

"Here's a container we're going to drop by parachute. Can you make a motorcycle that fits inside it?"

"Inside that? But it's only twelve inches wide!"

It's easy to imagine a conversation like this one being held at the Special Operations Executive design and research facility at Welwyn, England, during World War II. The British military wanted a motorcycle that could be stuffed inside a canister and dropped by parachute to Allied agents working behind enemy lines. They needed something that would give soldiers and saboteurs a quick way to get around.

The result was the Welbike, a 98cc, small-wheeled, folding motorcycle with 25-centimeter (10-inch) wheels, weighing just 32 kilograms (70 pounds). Supposedly capable of being ready for use within seconds of being pulled from its drop canister, the Welbike had a top speed of 50 kilometers (30 miles) per hour and a range of about 145 kilometers (90 miles) before running out of gas.

The U.S. military produced its own version of parachute-dropped, two-wheeled vehicle: the Cushman Airborne scooter. The Cushman didn't go inside a canister; the parachute clipped onto the scooter itself. The Cushman went into action with American airborne divisions during the D-Day invasion but the scooters proved unreliable and slow. Instead of being ridden by paratroopers, most wound up being used on military bases well behind the lines.

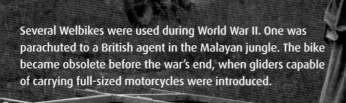

Several Welbikes were used during World War II. One was parachuted to a British agent in the Malayan jungle. The bike became obsolete before the war's end, when gliders capable of carrying full-sized motorcycles were introduced.

During the North African campaign, the U.S. Army commissioned both Indian and Harley-Davidson to manufacture a motorcycle that would stand up to the rigors of desert warfare. Both companies turned out similar vehicles: motorcycles that were shaft-driven, as opposed to being driven by a chain that would become clogged with sand. (Shaft-driven motorcycles weren't a new idea—Glenn Curtiss used one for his record-setting ride of 1907—but they weren't commonly built, because chain-driven motorcycles were cheaper to produce.) Although several hundred desert bikes were built by each company, they never saw combat. Long before they hit the deserts of North Africa, they were made redundant by another prototype military vehicle: the jeep.

In 1940, the U.S. military drew up specifications for a lightweight, four-wheel-drive "go anywhere" vehicle. The end result, in 1941, was the "General Purpose" vehicle—the GP ("jeep"). Its four wheels offered greater stability than a motorcycle, and it could tackle the same types of terrain. It could also carry more soldiers and supplies and could be mounted with larger weapons than a motorcycle sidecar.

Despite the development of the jeep, motorcycles were used by the hundreds of thousands during the war. Even wartime comic-book heroes mounted up. Captain America featured Steve Rogers, a 4-F military reject who was fed a "super soldier"

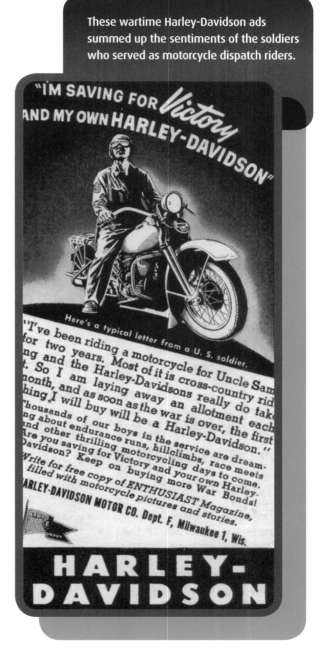

These wartime Harley-Davidson ads summed up the sentiments of the soldiers who served as motorcycle dispatch riders.

serum that turned him into the ultimate fighting machine. One 1943 comic shows "Cap"—together with his machine gun-toting sidekick, Bucky, riding pillion — leaping a motorcycle over Nazi troops while leading a charge of Russian tanks.

POST-WAR BLAHS

The companies that supplied the war effort were quick to point out to consumers what rugged products they'd built. Harley-Davidson's post-war advertising included numerous testimonials from motorcycle dispatch riders. As the ads said, "Harley-Davidson took a beating...and still kept on running."

On the home front, the company advertised how its motorcycles contributed to the war effort by minimizing gas and oil consumption. A 1942 ad boasted that Harley bikes did their "patriotic duty" by conserving essential products for military planes and tanks.

World War II gave many soldiers—both men and women—a taste for motorcycle riding. Those who served as dispatch riders enjoyed a freedom that many other soldiers lacked. Most of their duties involved riding alone, far from the scrutiny of officers. A delay caused by a visit to a sweetheart or a quick nap could easily be explained by tales of mechanical problems.

Once World War II was over, however, returning dispatch riders often had a hard time adjusting to civilian life. It seemed tame after a life of two-wheeled freedom mixed with the danger and excitement of combat.

STOP! **Long after World War II, films romanticized the independent spirit of the motorcycle rider. In one of the best-known scenes from the 1963 movie *The Great Escape*, Captain Virgil Hilts (played by Steve McQueen, who raced motorcycles when he wasn't acting) escapes a German prisoner of war camp then tries to jump his Triumph motorcycle over a barbed-wire fence. He's recaptured in the end, but his spirit remains unbroken.**

5 FUN AND GAMES

In Roman times, expert riders would harness up two horses, then gallop down the racetrack while standing with one foot on the back of each horse. In the 1800s, when Wild-West shows were popular, trick riders would hang off the saddle of a galloping horse or do a headstand on its back.

Riding a motorcycle through a wall of flame was a popular stunt in the 1940s. Daredevils like Cliff Majors, pictured here, inspired a later generation of stunt riders.

When the motorcycle came along, it gave trick riders a whole new way to perform stunts. On a motorcycle, trick riders could not only duplicate these stunts but could up the ante by doing things a horse couldn't, like leap into the air off a jump or race around the inside wall of a large circular drum.

Motorcycle trick riding first became popular in North America in the 1920s—the heyday of crazy stunts. Stunt riders crashed through flaming walls and jumped their motorcycles over obstacles, even a row of people lying side by side on the ground.

Inspired by the board tracks used for motorcycle racing, daredevils constructed a board track that was nothing but one big, banked curve. The "wall of death" was a large, wooden drum about six meters (20 feet) high and nine meters (30 feet)

The Mexico City Police drill team toured North America in 1928, performing stunts such as this human pyramid.

in diameter with a platform above for spectators. Used as a fairground attraction, it could be taken apart and moved from one county fair to the next. A motorcycle would race around the inside of the wall—the bike almost parallel with the ground below—held in place against the vertical walls by centrifugal force. To draw a crowd, some riders took a monkey or a lion along for the ride in a sidecar as an added attraction.

"SLANT ARTIST"

A motorcycle rider who competes in hill climb competitions.

DAREDEVILS ON FILM

The daredevil acts of this era translated well to the silver screen, where motorcycles could provide the action scenes audiences loved. These were the days before elaborate, computer-generated special effects. In the 1936 film *Crash Donovan*, a carnival stuntman joins the police and uses his motorcycle to chase down criminals. In a climactic scene, "Crash" rides his bike through flames to rescue a fellow cop. In reality, however, most motorcycle policemen spent their days chasing down speeders on the highways.

To moviegoers of the 1930s and 1940s, motorcycle racers and stunt riders might have seemed crazy, but the audience rooted for them. There was an occasional scene that showed the dangers of the sport—scenes of racers lying injured after a bad crash or a stunt gone wrong—but for the most part, the motorcyclists were portrayed as loveable underdogs. This

STOP! Today, motorcycle drill teams such as the Shriners ride in parades. So do the Seattle Cossacks, formed in 1938 by a group of motorcycle racers who named their team after the fierce Russian cavalrymen.

was especially true in the 1936 British film *No Limits*, in which a chimney sweep builds his own motorcycle from scratch and enters the famous Isle of Man Tourist Trophy race. He sets a new speed record—but only because his throttle gets stuck in the wide-open position.

STUNTS ON PARADE

As well as launching the careers of individual stunt riders, the 1920s, 1930s, and 1940s also gave rise to motorcycle drill teams. These riders dressed in matching uniforms and rode their motorcycles in formation, usually in parades. Many of

All Dressed Up and Somewhere to Go

In the 1930s and 1940s motorcycle clubs were springing up everywhere. Many had uniforms reminiscent of those worn by high-school marching bands. Members wore high boots, military-style jodhpurs (pants flared from knee to hip) with a stripe running down the side of each leg, and either a shirt and tie or a western-style shirt like those worn in rodeos, embroidered with the club name. Peak caps were popular—a fashion trend that may have been inspired by caps worn by motorcycle cops, or those worn by World War I motorcycle dispatch riders.

In 1939 more than 2,000 motorcycle club members attended the New York World's Fair, where a prize was awarded to the best-dressed club.

The uniforms worn by the Corpus Christi Sea Horses motorcycle club auxiliary of 1941 were typical of the time. Rival motorcycle clubs used to compete for best-dressed awards.

their stunts were relatively tame: riding in a circle, nose to tail with the bike ahead, or crisscrossing two lines of motorcycles. Other tricks took a lot of skill. Half a dozen riders might climb onto a single machine, then hang from the front, back, and sides of it by their feet. Or they might form a human pyramid on top of two motorcycles riding side-by-side. Other stunts involved the rider steering the bike while balancing on top of a ladder that was strapped to the motorcycle.

Police departments and armies also got into the act, forming their own motorcycle drill teams. The White Helmets motorcycle display team, made up of members of Britain's Royal Signals Corps, formed in 1927 as a recruiting tool.

Its organizers hoped that people would be thrilled by the daring displays and want to join the army. The team is still going strong today. Its uniformed riders—all wearing white helmets—perform high-speed stunts on British Triumphs. They crash through burning walls, jump over automobiles, and ride facing backwards while sitting on the handlebars and juggling.

EVERYDAY DARING

Ordinary motorcyclists were having fun of a tamer variety. By 1924 a national organization for riders had formed—the American Motorcycle Association (AMA). It helped local motorcycle clubs keep in touch with each other and organized group rides known as "gypsy tours." These early rallies encouraged entire families to ride out into the country for a weekend of picnicking and camping.

Members of a motorcycle club head off to a rally in 1947.

Gypsy tours gave people the opportunity to dream up goofy new things to do with their motorcycles. Home movies show riders pushing their bikes by the handlebars in a backwards race, or riding around with balloons tied to their bikes and a passenger riding pillion on the back. The passengers would try to pop the other motorcyclists' balloons with sticks, and the rider with the last unbroken balloon tied to his motorcycle was the winner. There were also "slow races" in which the last rider across the finish line was the winner—anyone who stalled or put a foot to the ground was disqualified.

This ad shows what a well-dressed rider wore when off on a "gypsy tour."

A typical gypsy tour might include a game of motorcycle polo, or a "poker run" in which riders stopped at checkpoints to collect cards. At the end of the run, riders would compare their cards to see who had the best poker hand. There were also competitions such as hill climbing and plank riding. When it was all over, participants got a commemorative watch fob or pin.

Gypsy-tour participants might make a lot of noise as they pushed a beer barrel around on the beach with the front wheels of their bikes, but they weren't seen as a threat to anyone. As one hotel owner, whose hometown in Washington State was the site of a gypsy tour, commented, "Oh, these guys aren't near as bad as the loggers." Back in the 1930s and 1940s, loggers—men who worked in the bush for months on end, then came into town to drink and get rowdy—were considered the troublemakers, not motorcycle racers.

Dot Robinson was one of many women who competed in endurance races. Here, she and a fellow racer struggle through slippery gravel during the 1952 Lumberjack Run in Michigan.

NOT JUST THE LADIES' AUXILIARY

Women motorcycle riders were few and far between in those days. Most women rode pillion—behind their husbands or boyfriends—and belonged to the ladies' auxiliary of the motorcycle club. But there were exceptions. One of these was Linda Dugeau, who began riding motorcycles in her teens in the early 1930s. After hearing about the "Ninety-Nines," an

Slant Artists

Hill climbs were a popular part of many gypsy-tour rallies. In these competitions, still held today, riders take turns trying to make it to the top of a steep hill. Each rider takes off from a standing start at the bottom of the hill and tries to reach the top in the shortest time. Some of the hills are so steep that spectators can't stand upright on them and bikes that do make it to the top have to be lowered using a rope and pulley. Known as "slant artists," hill climbers use motorcycles equipped with chains on their rear wheels. The bikes are so powerful that they would do a wheelie and flip if ridden by someone who didn't know how to handle them.

The Family Motorcycle

The 1933 movie *Duck Soup*, starring the renowned comedians, the Marx Brothers, had a running gag that involved a motorcycle sidecar. In one scene, Groucho and Harpo drive off on their motorcycle and leave the sidecar behind. Later in the film, the gag gets better when the sidecar drives off and leaves the motorcycle behind. In another scene, the motorcycle is triumphantly announced as "the emperor's new car." Everyone got the joke—sidecars were for people who couldn't afford an automobile, not for emperors.

Until the 1910s, motorcycles were cheaper than automobiles. A 1909 Harley sold for $210—one-quarter of the $850 price of a Model T touring car. Families with kids and not much money would buy a sidecar-equipped motorcycle. Richer families, meanwhile, could enjoy the luxury of an automobile, with roll-up windows to keep out the rain and a heater to keep them warm in winter. A car in the garage became a status symbol, while the motorcycle was something the working classes rode.

By the late 1920s, however, the assembly line that Henry Ford introduced in 1908 meant that more affordable automobiles could give the motorcycle a run for its money. By 1927, the cost of a Model T touring car had dropped to $380, a price that put it in direct competition with the motorcycle-and-sidecar combination as the cheap form of family transportation. Across the Atlantic, the compact and inexpensive Austin 7 automobile created a similar challenge for the British motorcycle industry by the end of the 1920s.

Rarely seen today, sidecars are typically used for long-distance touring.

The Bean family of Washington State pile into a motorcycle sidecar for a family outing in the 1920s.

organization of female pilots, Dugeau decided to found a similar group for female motorcyclists. She wrote to motorcycle dealerships and women whose names had appeared in motorcycle magazines. In 1940 she formed the "Motor Maids."

During the 1940s the Motor Maids paraded at AMA national races. They wore a uniform that was typical of motorcycle clubs of the era, with a few feminine touches: gray slacks with blue piping, a royal blue blouse—and ladylike white gloves. The club is still in existence—although these days, members tend to wear jeans and club T-shirts.

Dorothy "Dot" Robinson, a co-founder of the Motor Maids, was also an accomplished endurance rider. In 1937

"RIDING PILLION"
Riding as a passenger on the back of a motorcycle.

she came second in the two-day Jack Pine Enduro race in Michigan—when more than half the competitors failed to even finish. In 1940 she won the race. But rather than congratulate her, the AMA secretary banned women from the event. Robinson drafted a petition and got AMA

STOP Some sidecars were very elaborate. The Scott Sociable of 1919 was an enclosed sidecar made of wood. The "Seal" sidecar, with its windshield and cloth roof, was more like a car with an attached motorcycle that had been stripped of its handlebars. This awkward-looking vehicle was guided by the passenger using a steering wheel, while the person sitting on the motorcycle changed gears. Built from 1910 to the early 1930s, the Seal was advertised as "sociable, economical and light."

members to sign, and, as a result, the rule was struck down.

Robinson could ride hard, but she also prided herself on being a lady. After a race, she would clean up and put on makeup before coming down to join the other racers in the bar, wearing a black sheath dress and pillbox hat. Over the course of her life she owned several motorcycles, all of them painted pink.

GOING SOLO

Not all motorcyclists belonged to clubs and rode in rallies. Some struck out on their own, looking for adventure and fun. One of these was Bessie "BB" Stringfield, who started riding in the late 1920s. At the age of 19 she began tossing a penny onto a map and riding to wherever it landed. During the 1930s and 1940s she rode through all 48 mainland U.S. states, as well as through Europe, Brazil, and Haiti. Because she was black, she often had trouble finding a place to stay. Sometimes, she'd pull over to a filling station, lay her jacket on the handlebars, and sleep right there on her bike. She also did hill climbing and trick riding, and for a time worked in carnival stunt shows.

The trophy for the Death's Head Derby was made from a human skull. The Olympia Motorcycle Club got the skull from a local Washington state dental school, where dentistry students had once practiced on its teeth. Gene Thiessen, pictured here, won the grisly trophy in 1953.

Over in England, there was Theresa Wallach, a British woman who competed in trials, scrambles, and road race events. In 1939 Wallach won a Gold Star at Brooklands racetrack, an award given to any rider who managed to complete a lap at 160 kilometers (100 miles) per hour. Despite bad weather—it was pouring rain on the day Wallach made her lap—she was clocked just over the required speed. Wallach tried to join a motorcycle club, but they didn't want any women members. During the 1930s, when she was winning competitions, her parents told her to keep the trophies out of sight, because ladies didn't ride motorcycles.

In 1935, together with Florence Blenkiron, Wallach rode a sidecar-equipped, 600cc Panther motorcycle from London, England, to Cape Town, South

Bessie Stringfield began riding when she was 16. Over the course of her life she completed eight solo cross-country tours of the U.S., and she was the founder of the Iron Horse Motorcycle Club. She died in 1993, but her legacy lives on in clubs such as Sisters With a Throttle (SWAT), a club for African-American women based in Washington, DC.

Three-Wheeled Trucks

During the Depression of the 1930s very few people had money to spend. Motorcycle manufacturers had to scramble to find new markets. Sidecars had lost out to warm and dry automobile interiors as a means of transporting the family, but there was one vehicle the motorcycle could still compete with: the delivery truck. All the designers had to do was add a third wheel. Indian's "Traffic Car" was a three-wheeled vehicle that looked like a motorcycle on the front half, and a small delivery truck on the rear.

Indian also produced a three-wheeled motorcycle for servicing stranded vehicles, as well as one for police and fire departments. "Outperforms any four-wheeled vehicle over rugged terrain," the ads for the latter boasted. "Perfect for forest fire patrols with plenty of room for emergency equipment."

Africa. They were the first motorcyclists—male or female—to cross the Sahara Desert on a motorcycle. They rode from oasis to oasis, at times arguing with the French Foreign Legion for permission to continue their journey; the legion didn't feel it was proper for women to be traveling on their own, especially on motorcycles. They rebuilt the engine once, and at one point had to push the motorcycle more than 40 kilometers (25 miles) when it broke down. Wallach wrote a book about the journey, *The Rugged Road*.

Long-distance journeys might be grueling, but for these early motorcycle riders, that was all part of the fun and adventure of seeing the world on two wheels.

Harley-Davidson's most popular three-wheeled vehicle was the Servicar, which had a storage compartment between the two rear wheels. This photo shows Chicago police officers on their Servicars in 1951.

8 BAD BOYS ON BIKES

If you ever talk to a Hells Angel, don't make the mistake of calling him a member of a motorcycle gang.

"It's a club," he'll tell you. "A motorcycle club."

To many people who don't ride, any group of guys on loud motorcycles equals a "gang." Just say the word "bikers," and people immediately think of bad dudes who look grungy and cause trouble. They're dangerous and violent—people to be feared. No father would want his daughter dating one. No matter how clean-cut a guy might be, if he shows up on a motorcycle he always gets a sideways look, if not from dad, then from the neighbors.

Pictures of skulls, wings, swords, and flames help create the "bad boy" imagery of biker style.

How did motorcycle riders get such a bad rep?

Up until the mid-1940s there might be the occasional complaint about loud exhaust pipes, but otherwise things were pretty tame. All of this changed in 1947, when spit and polish gave way to grease and booze.

On a Fourth-of-July weekend in 1947 the small California town of Hollister played host to an AMA gypsy tour that featured a race and hill climb event. As well as the 1,500 motorcycle riders registered in these competitions, an estimated 3,000 more riders showed up to watch the race—and to party. These included members of motorcycle clubs with names like the Boozefighters, Pissed Off Bastards, Winos, Satan's Sinners, Galloping Ghosts, Market Street Commandos, 13 Rebels and Yellow Jackets. Several got drunk and raced their bikes up and down the street, threw beer bottles out of hotel windows, or rode their bikes into the town's bars and restaurants. Dozens were arrested, but the rest overwhelmed the town's seven-man police department. According to news reports,

I SIGNED THE PLEDGE FOR

MUFFLER MIKE

QUIET RIDING

In the 1940s "outlaw" motorcycle clubs began to get a lot of bad publicity. The American Motorcycle Association fought back with campaigns that encouraged riders to behave responsibly. In 1948 riders began signing a pledge with the AMA to keep their machines quiet. In return they were given "Muffler Mike" stickers, complete with white spaces where each rider could sign his or her name.

40 state police, armed with tear gas, had to be called in to restore order. Dozens of people were injured.

There had been rowdiness and fistfights at motorcycle club events before, but Hollister was the one that really made the news. *Life* magazine ran a photo of one of the carousing bikers, though later it was said that the photographer posed the shot. The biker is shown leaning back on his bike, beer bottle in hand, clothes mussed, with a boozy expression on his face, in a street littered with beer bottles. The caption announced that motorcyclists had "terrorized" the town. The next year, a similar "cycle riot" in Riverside, California, prompted that town's sheriff to describe the motorcyclists as "hoodlums."

The outlaw motorcycle club was born.

The bad press generated by the outlaw clubs didn't sit well with the AMA. In 1948 its secretary, Lin A. Kuchler, commented that "the disreputable cyclists are possibly one percent of the total number

"TATS"
(or "tatties")
Tattoos.

of motorcyclists; only one percent are hoodlums and troublemakers."

The outlaw clubs reveled in their bad-boy image, proudly wearing diamond-shaped patches stitched with the words "one percenter."

The AMA worked hard to present motorcycling in the best light possible. At the Laconia races in 1947 it reminded participants to conduct themselves in a "gentlemanly manner." In 1948 the AMA launched a "muffler Mike" campaign that urged riders to keep their machines quiet. A 1961 "Put Your Best Wheel Forward" campaign asked riders to "present a good appearance to the public" by dressing

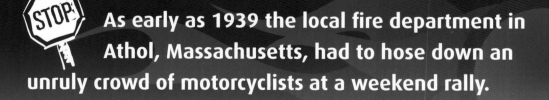

As early as 1939 the local fire department in Athol, Massachusetts, had to hose down an unruly crowd of motorcyclists at a weekend rally.

"PROSPECT"

Potential motorcycle club member.

presentably, riding safely, and respecting quiet zones.

For a time, the campaigns worked. Despite Hollister, most people recognized that only a few motorcyclists were bad apples. Outlaw bikers were seen as boozers and losers—hardly people you'd want to emulate.

Then, in 1953, *The Wild One* roared onto the silver screen.

CALL OF THE WILD

The Wild One glamorized what had happened in Hollister and delivered a bad-boy biker that guys wanted to be like and girls

The 1953 movie *The Wild One* helped make motorcyles exciting and cool for a new generation of riders. The film featured a young Marlon Brando as Johnny, the leader of the Black Rebels Motorcycle Club.

wished they could kiss: Marlon Brando. Brando, in a black leather jacket and peak cap, stars as Johnny, leader of the Black Rebels Motorcycle Club. He's handsome. He's cool. He rides a motorcycle.

The film also included a character that real-life outlaw bikers could identify with—Lee Marvin, as Chino, leader of a rival motorcycle gang, The Beetles.

Trailers for *The Wild One* promised "a gang of hot-riding hot heads who ride into, terrorize and take over a town." The film delivered. The Black Rebels drag race down the main street, fight with The Beetles, bust up the town, and intimidate the locals. And for no good reason. When Johnny's asked what he's rebelling against, he utters the now-famous reply: "What've you got?"

The Wild One forged a link between motorcycles and lawlessness—and added

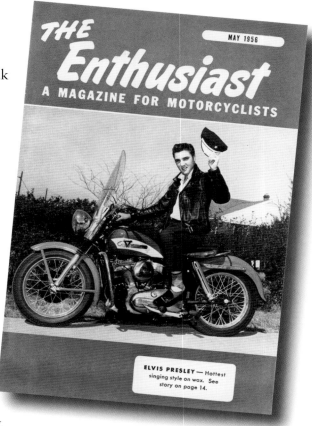

Everyone wanted to wear a black leather jacket after seeing Marlon Brando in *The Wild One*. This issue of the Harley-Davidson *Enthusiast* featured Elvis Presley wearing the jacket that had become as much a part of sex appeal as rock 'n' roll music.

STOP **"Wino" Willy Forkner of the Boozefighters Motorcycle Club was said to be the inspiration for Chino, the rival gang leader in *The Wild One*.**

A Patchy Beginning

When the first motorcycle clubs formed, they decorated their shirts, sweaters, and jackets with cloth patches embroidered with the name of the club. Clubs that were sanctioned by the AMA wore a patch with their club initials and the letters "MC" (motorcycle club) wrapped around the AMA logo.

The outlaw motorcycle clubs of the late 1940s also liked to write their names on their jackets. Their club names were rougher, however, and so were their club logos: skulls, flames, devils—the same symbols you find in biker tattoo art today. Many of these symbols were inspired by U.S. Air Force unit patches of World War II, which emphasized the toughness of the squadron and the death their planes would rain upon the enemy. According to Hells Angel "Sonny" Barger, the famous "death's head" design of the club's patch—a winged skull in an aviator's helmet—was inspired by a military patch found in a surplus store in 1957.

The "colors" of a motorcycle club identify the wearer as either friend or foe. Over the years, these colors came to have a standardized form. There's a logo-like symbol in the middle, with curved bars of text, known as "rockers," above and below it. The top rocker gives the name of the club, the bottom, the city, state or country where the club is located. There's also a small square with the letters "MC."

The colors are most often sewn on the back of a denim jacket whose sleeves have been hacked off—a practical modification in hot and sunny California, birthplace of the Hells Angels.

Tattoos, leather and chains: these Los Bravos motorcycle club members wear a look that instantly declares their membership and status in the club.

sex appeal. It introduced what would later become a standard character in biker movies: the small-town girl who's seduced by a big-city biker. The formula was set: bad boy plus bike equals babes. Every guy wanted to ride a motorcycle and look tough.

The 1957 movie *Motorcycle Gang* tried to capitalize on *The Wild One*'s success, but the motorcycle club it focuses on—the Sky Riders—are clean-cut kids in spotless white T-shirts who never get their hands dirty, even when tuning their bikes. The film did, however, dramatize the growing split between "legitimate" motorcycle clubs and their bastard twins, the outlaw bikers.

THE HELLS ANGELS

The same year the AMA made its one percent pronouncement, the Hells Angels Motorcycle Club was formed in California.

"COLORS"

Clothing that bears motorcycle club patches, usually denim or leather jackets or vests.

They weren't the first outlaw club. Nor would they be the last. But theirs was the club that would become known worldwide. The first Hells Angels chapter was formed in San Bernardino ("Berdoo") by members of the Pissed Off Bastards of Bloomington. The second chapter was in San Francisco, and was partially made up of Market Street Commandos (also of Hollister fame). Other California chapters

STOP Although most of the early outlaw motorcycle clubs were Caucasian, there were exceptions. The East Bay Dragons was founded in Oakland, California, in the late 1950s by African-American Tobie Gene Levingston, at a time when, as he put it, "it was a revolutionary act for a black man to ride a Harley chopper."

quickly followed. By 1966 the club had expanded outside of California as other, originally independent, motorcycle clubs were accepted into the Hells Angels and became patch-wearing members.

When they first began, the Hells Angels were just a bunch of working-class guys in their early 20s who liked to ride motorcycles and drink beer. And they weren't the only motorcycle club that grew to have an international membership. How did they become a household name, when other outlaw motorcycle clubs such as the Boozefighters—a club that also formed in the 1940s and which is also still around today—did not?

"CITIZEN"

Everyone not in an outlaw club. Outlaw club members borrowed this term from newspaper accounts that contrasted "riff-raff" bikers with upstanding citizens and townsfolk.

Today, the Hells Angels Motorcycle Club (HAMC) has chapters in North and South America, Australia and New Zealand, South Africa, and 17 European countries, and is estimated to have more than 2,000 members.

According to journalist Hunter S. Thompson, who hung out with the Hells Angels in 1965 and 1966 and wrote a book about them, the club was virtually unknown—except, that is, to local police—until the mid-1960s. Then everything exploded. As Thompson put it, "the Hells Angels as they exist today were virtually created by *Time*, *Newsweek* and the *New York Times*."

The publicity started with a low rumble as early as 1957 when yet another AMA event went sour. It happened at Angels Camp, California, where the AMA was hosting a gypsy tour and dirt-track racing event. Two Hells Angels who were street racing lost control of their bikes on a curve and crashed into a group of other motorcyclists. Two people died and three were injured—one of them had his foot "torn off," according to a newspaper account.

In 1964, in Monterey, California, two members of the Hells Angels were arrested on charges of raping two teenage girls. California politicians demanded that something be done about the outlaw club. The result was a government enquiry called the Lynch Report.

Released in March 1965, the Lynch Report really put the Hells Angels in the spotlight. Prepared by California's attorney general, it included a long list of the

Biker World

They've even heard of the Hells Angels in the former Soviet Union. In Russia, the Nochniye Volki (Night Wolves) ride chopped motorcycles, wear black leather, and listen to Motörhead. Their patch—a wolf's head trailing flames—is styled after the Hells Angels death's head.

Like the American bikers whose culture they've embraced, the Night Wolves are fiercely patriotic. They're proud of their Russian-built Ural motorcycles. When Ural wanted to release a custom motorcycle, the Night Wolves collaborated on the design. The result was the Wolf. With its raked front forks, it looks like it rolled straight out of 1960s California.

In the Philippines, the Mad Dog Motorcycle Club has a snarling bulldog in a spiked collar as its club colors (club patch) under a red-and-white "rocker" (an arch bearing the name of the club). With their tattoos, black leather, and bandanas, the Mad Dogs look like American bikers on their choppers. They tend to make the news because they ride fast and loud, and because they support a local orphanage.

This Man May Save Your Life!

Rebels weren't the only ones riding motorcycles. The law was riding them, too. The building of interstate highways got into high gear in the 1950s and, as more and more people hit the road, the number of auto-related injuries and fatalities climbed. Motorcycles—which could weave in and out of traffic—were the ideal vehicle to help police get to the scene of an accident.

At GREAT DANGER to his own life and limb, he patrols the highway to curb reckless, careless and drunken drivers—killers whose victims number more than 36,000 killed and 1,500,000 injured in the past year.

His very presence lessens *your* danger—increases *your* safety—may save *your* life. He deserves your respect and co-operation.

He plays a major role in the great Crusade For Traffic Safety to solve what the President of the United States calls "a national problem of first importance".

Taking an active part in this crusade are the capital stock fire and casualty insurance companies. Their traffic experts help communities study specific problems and eliminate the causes of mounting accidents.

Yes—safety on our highways is everybody's responsibility! Join the Crusade For Traffic Safety and save a life—maybe your own!

For the name of a nearby America Fore agent call Western Union by number and ask for Operator 25.

America Fore
★ INSURANCE GROUP ★

★ The Continental Insurance Company
★ Niagara Fire Insurance Company
★ The Fidelity and Casualty Company of New York
★ Fidelity-Phenix Fire Insurance Company
★ American Eagle Fire Insurance Company

"hoodlum activities" of outlaw motorcycle clubs. According to the report, these clubs were involved in drug trafficking, theft, assault, and rape.

Newspapers across the U.S. picked up the story, putting the Hells Angels name in headlines. So did national magazines such as *Time* and *Newsweek*. Lurid stories involving the Hells Angels, taken from the Lynch Report, were told over and over, including the 1963 "invasion" of Porterville, California, in which rampaging bikers—some of whom may have been Hells Angels—pawed local women and beat up an old man.

The Hells Angels themselves obligingly provided yet more fodder for the press. That October, Oakland chapter members waded into an anti-Vietnam War demonstration and punched out protesters. When the chapter later released a statement about how its members felt compelled to take a stand against "un-American activity," the press ate it up. The Oakland chapter even wrote a letter to the U.S. president, volunteering for behind-the-lines service against the Viet Cong.

The president didn't take them up on it.

The Hells Angels gained lasting infamy in December of 1969 when they were hired—for $500 worth of beer—to provide security at a Rolling Stones concert at the Altamont Speedway in California, part of the Let It Bleed tour. According to Ralph "Sonny" Barger, then president of the Oakland chapter, the concert audience turned nasty, throwing beer bottles at the Hells Angels' bikes, and club members

"OLD LADIES"

Girlfriends of bikers.

beat up three people in retaliation. Then, during the song "Under My Thumb," one of the fans drew a gun. The Hells Angels jumped him. Eighteen-year-old Meredith Hunter was fatally stabbed. The whole tragic incident was captured on film in the 1970 concert movie *Gimme Shelter*. Although one Hells Angels member was charged with murder, a jury acquitted him on the grounds of self-defense, since Hunter had a gun. For years, there were rumors that a second Hells Angel had also stabbed Hunter, inflicting the fatal wounds, but in 2005 police reviewed the film footage, decided that only one Hells Angel did the stabbing, and formally closed the case.

BAD BOYS ON FILM

When the director of *Terminator 2: Judgment Day* wanted to show how tough Arnold Schwarzenegger's cyborg character was, he had the Terminator walk into a bar and beat up some bikers, then steal one of their motorcycles. Movie audiences instantly understood what was going on. No biker gives up his motorcycle without a fight. Like the proverbial rifle, it would have to be pried out of the biker's cold, dead hand.

The Terminator kicks the bikers' butts without even blinking—and frightens them so badly they don't even have the guts to shoot him in the back as he rides away on the stolen Harley.

Now that's tough.

Motorcycles may equal menace these days, but that wasn't always the case. In the early 1960s, even after the release of *The Wild One*, they were still occasionally portrayed as something to laugh at. The "beach party" movies of 1963 to 1966 featured the Rats, a bumbling motorcycle gang led by Eric von Zipper. Everything that Johnny of *The Wild One* was, von Zipper was not. They both dressed in black leather, but one was cool and the other was a fool.

Soon, however, the beach party films drifted off with the surf. *The Wild Angels* hit the theaters and the motorcycle gang movie was born.

This 1966 film included actual members of the Hells Angels in its cast—and more swastikas than a Nazi rally. It told the story of Loser, a member of a motorcycle club called the Angels, who is shot after he steals a police motorcycle. His funeral turns into a free-for-all after the Angels' leader, Blues (played by Peter Fonda), gets into a shouting match with the preacher.

When the preacher asks what they want, Blues answers, "We want to be free to ride our machines without being hassled by the man. And we want to get loaded. And we want to have a good time." The Angels proceed to do just that, wreaking havoc before fleeing in a cowardly fashion when police sirens wail.

The Hells Angels didn't like how *The Wild Angels* depicted them, but the moviegoing public did. Anything with "hell" or "angels" in the title was a guaranteed money-maker. Most people wouldn't want to meet the Hells Angels in person, but they were fascinated by seeing them on film. The bikers were a new kind of

"LID"

Helmet.

villain—something different from the standard Mafia gangster. Movies capitalized on their strange clothes, long hair, and shocking behavior, all of which had an almost freak-show appeal.

Over the next five years, literally dozens of biker films followed. As the films sought to one-up each other, no deed was too extreme or too vile. A movie biker would sell his "old lady" for a pack of cigarettes, beat up tourists and torch their campers, rape teenage girls and pregnant women and whip their boyfriends with motorcycle chains, or smoke dope and roar down sidewalks on his chopper,

STOP **After *The Wild Angels* was released, the Hells Angels sued director Roger Corman and American International Pictures for $2 million. They later settled out of court for $2,000.**

scattering small-town "citizens" like startled chickens. From time to time the bikers might save someone from a collapsed mine shaft or help oppressed Natives reclaim their ancestral lands, but deep down, they were still bad guys. Although some of the movie scenes were based on real-life horror stories, others were pure fiction. Biker movies helped define what a "biker" looked like: scraggly beard, filthy denim jacket with the sleeves cut off, long greasy hair, tattoos, and heavy black boots. More than three decades later—in countries around the world—that image endures.

The design of the classic motorcycle jacket we know today was heavily influenced by those worn by military bomber crews during World War II. Earlier motorcycle jackets in the 1920s were brown, but black proved to be a more practical color because it disguised oil stains. While the first motorcycle jackets had buttons, the diagonal zipper, which was easier to open and close while wearing riding gloves, came to be the norm.

America's finest line!

GENUINE BLACK HORSEHIDE
Motorcycle APPAREL
for Men and Women

• MADE RIGHT!
• PRICED RIGHT!
• STYLED RIGHT!

Jackets, shirts, pants and breeches . . . in a complete range of styles and sizes. All items are superbly tailored from selected black garment horsehide. Soft—pliable— durable . . . and always smart looking! No other line offers you more in features, comfort and utility. Look for the Buco label when you buy!

For FREE 1952 BUCO Catalog
ask your dealer or write to . . .

JOSEPH BUEGELEISEN CO.
1302 East Woodbridge   •   Detroit 7, Michigan
LARGEST MANUFACTURERS OF MOTORCYCLE ACCESSORIES IN THE U. S. A.

7 THE "NICEST PEOPLE"

Bike Week in Daytona, Florida, 2002. Out behind the Last Resort bar, a group of bikers gathers. One by one, they take turns with a sledgehammer, smashing a Japanese-built motorcycle. After the last one's had his turn and the bike is a mangled mess, it's strung up in a tree by a rope to the sound of cheers.

An adventurous Honda rider attempts a standing start at the top of the largest sand dune in the Simpson Desert of Central Australia. The sand dune is notable enough to have its own name: "Big Red," or Nappanerica.

This postcard, mailed in 1919, shows a motorcycle parked out front of the Iwai, a "Western food" restaurant in Sapporo, Japan. The man seated on the bike sports a Western-style suit and hat, but others in the photo are dressed in more traditional Japanese styles.

The bar's infamous hanging garden has claimed another "rice burner."

For many North American motorcycle riders, the gulf between a Japanese bike and an American bike is as wide as the Pacific. Those who prefer "American iron" sneer at Japanese bikes. Those who ride Japanese motorcycles can't imagine why anyone would put up with what they consider to be a lesser technology.

In the words of American motorcycle designer Craig Vetter, Americans like to build bikes "big and simple." The Japanese companies build them "small and complicated." And the Japanese, he grudgingly admits, build them better.

Is the attitude toward Japanese bikes simple jealousy, or is there something deeper at work here?

In 1912 Harley-Davidson started selling motorcycles in Japan—the American company's first exports to a foreign country. By 1925 the Japanese were snapping up about a thousand Harleys each year. Then came the Depression in 1929. Harley-Davidson was hit hard; by 1932 production at its Milwaukee factory had shrunk to just 10 percent of what it had been.

To help ease the sting, Harley-Davidson sold to the Sankyo Seiyako Corporation the tools and licensing rights needed to build lookalike motorcycles in Japan.

YOU MEET THE NICEST PEOPLE ON A HONDA

Maybe it's the incredibly low price, $245 (plus a modest set-up charge). Or the fact it doesn't gulp gas. Just sips it — 200 miles to the gallon. Or the way the masterful 4-stroke 50cc OHV engine carries you along at 45 mph without a murmur.

Or it could be the ease of 3-speed transmission, automatic clutch and the extra safety of Honda's cam-type brakes on both wheels. The optional push-button starter makes you feel right at home, too.

But most likely it's the fun. Evidently nothing catches on like the fun of owning a Honda. You see so many around these days. And the nicest people riding them. Merry Christmas. For address of your nearest dealer or other information, write: Dept. AA, American Honda Motor Co., Inc., 100 West Alondra, Gardena, Calif.

HONDA — world's biggest seller!

Honda developed the slogan "You meet the nicest people on a Honda" in 1962. The catch phrase was an attempt to clean up the image of motorcycling and make it attractive to people who ordinarily wouldn't try riding. The campaign paid off. By 1963, sales of Hondas in the U.S. had reached 150,000.

The end result was the Rikuo (Land King), built with Harley-Davidson technology. Money from the deal helped Harley-Davidson through the Depression, but the rise of a military government in Japan soured the relationship by the mid-1930s, and the license wasn't renewed. The Japanese continued to build motor-cycles using the machine tools Harley-Davidson had provided, however, until the early 1960s. Rikuos were even used by the Japanese army during World War II.

But the American market had new worries. In the decades following the war, the tide would turn. Instead of America selling motorcycles to Japan, the reverse would happen. It started as a trickle, but soon became a tsunami.

The Honda "minitrail" CT 70 was a pioneer among mini motorbikes and trail bikes. It was compact enough to fit in the trunk of a car.

HOW IT STARTED IN JAPAN

After World War II, Japan faced tough times. The nation's train system was disrupted and gas shortages made driving a car problematic. Commuters turned to two-wheeled transportation. There were plenty of military-surplus parts around, including small engines that could be mounted on bicycles. That's how Soichiro Honda got his start. In 1946 he began producing motorized bicycles with war-surplus engines. Soon he began building his own engines.

The American soldiers who occupied Japan after the war brought the first Hondas back to North America in the early 1950s. It wasn't until 1958, however, that direct imports began, starting in Vancouver, BC.

In 1959, the year that American Honda Motors opened in Los Angeles, Americans were only buying

STOP By 1949 Soichiro Honda's company was manufacturing entire motorcycles, including a 98cc two-cylinder bike he called the Dream. It was a boxy-looking, utilitarian vehicle, but it was just what the Japanese needed to get around.

about 50,000 to 60,000 motorcycles a year—one-tenth the number of bikes that were being sold in Japan each year (the Japanese automobile industry was still just getting started in the 1950s). Few North Americans used motorcycles as their primary vehicles. If they wanted to get around, they bought a car. Honda set out to change that.

The company ran ads in *Life* magazine that showed homemakers, kids, and businessmen in suits riding Honda motorbikes. The ads shied away from using the word "motorcycle," using only product names instead.

Something to Sing About

In the early 1960s California record producer Gary Usher capitalized on Honda's popularity by putting together a studio group to sing motorcycle songs. He was originally going to name the group The Rising Sons, but settled on The Hondells, instead.

The Hondells released their first album in 1964. It featured songs with titles like "Black Denim," "My Little Bike," "Lay It Down," "Cycle Chase," and "Honda Holiday." The group also released a top-ten single, "Little Honda," written by Brian Wilson of the Beach Boys (who would include the song on one of their own albums that year). The Honda company had nothing to do with the formation of the Hondells—and, according to one of the singers, may have been considering a lawsuit over the use of the name. Honda later commissioned a song of its own from another record producer, Mike Curb: "You Meet the Nicest People on a Honda."

The Hondells

CYCLE CHASE · YOU'RE GONNA' RIDE WITH ME · NIGHT RIDER · THE LONELY RIDER · MY BUDDY SEAT · BLACK DENIM · LAY IT DOWN
MY BIKE · HE WASN'T COMING BACK · THE SIDEWINDER   THE REBEL (WITHOUT A CAUSE) · HONDA HOLIDAY

Mercury RECORDS

MERCURY HI-FIDELITY MG 2098

Honda's North American sales staff was instructed to wear suits. Mechanics were ordered to keep their uniforms spotless. It helped that Honda's engines, unlike those of American or British built bikes, didn't drip oil onto showroom floors. The motorcycle industry was cleaning up its act.

BIRTH OF THE SUPERBIKE

After Honda led the way, a number of other Japanese companies were quick to jump into the North American market. These businesses weren't motorcycle manufacturers to begin with, however—not even close. Yamaha started out making pianos and organs—its logo is three tuning forks in a circle. The company only diversified to include motorcycles in 1955, but was selling them in the U.S. by 1960. Suzuki built weaving looms before World War II. They made their first "motorcycle" in 1952—a bicycle with a motor attached. Eleven years later they were selling proper motorcycles in North America. Kawasaki was originally an aircraft manufacturer. After merging with the Meguro motorcycle company in 1963, they opened an office in the U.S. in 1965.

Two professional racers, nearly neck and neck, take a steep corner in a racetrack.

Until the 1960s, the Japanese had been scorned as "copyists." A "made in Japan" label meant inferior quality, no matter what the product. But North American riders quickly acknowledged the technical superiority of Japanese-built motorcycles.

Harley-Davidson—the only surviving U.S. motorcycle manufacturer after 1953—wasn't too worried about the Japanese bikes, though. The Japanese had a reputation for turning out cute bikes with small engines, like its best seller, the Super Cub (or Honda 50 as it was known in the U.S.).

The real competition, so the American manufacturers thought, came from across the Atlantic—from the British, who built large-engine bikes that were lighter but could match an American motorcycle, or even beat it, in terms of speed and performance.

Everyone thought the Japanese couldn't build a big bike.

"RICE ROCKET"
(or Rice burner)
A Japanese motorcycle.

They were wrong.

The first hint of trouble was the Honda CB450 "Black Bomber," introduced in 1965. It had an electric starter (at a time when kick starts were still standard), cost less than American or British bikes, was more reliable, and had a top speed that left larger-engined Harleys in its dust. The body blow was struck three years later. In 1968, Honda introduced the Honda CB750, capable of a top speed of 193 kilometers (120 miles) per hour—this

Honda's "cute" reputation was reinforced with the release of their "monkey bikes," which supposedly got their name because adult riders looked like monkeys when they perched on them. They had gutless 49cc engines, fold-down handlebars, tiny five-inch wheels, a cartoonish red-and-white paint job and tartan-pattern seats.

Hollywood Hondas

Honda motorcycles also made inroads into Hollywood. In the 1964 movie *Roustabout*, Elvis plays a motorcycle-riding carnival worker. In one scene Elvis is confronted by three college boys who mock his choice of bike: a Honda 350cc "sickle."

One taunts him, asking why American motorcycles aren't "good enough."

Things degenerate into a fight, and Elvis whips two of the students. The third protests that Elvis is using karate moves.

Elvis grins. "That goes with the sickle."

In real life, however, Elvis rode Harley-Davidsons. A 1956 photograph shows him brooding over his bike in a classic *Wild One* pose.

during a decade when just reaching 160 kilometers (100 miles) per hour was a big deal for British machines.

The superbike was born.

Other Japanese manufacturers quickly followed the CB750's lead. The larger Japanese bikes had better acceleration and handling than American or British bikes of comparable engine size, and didn't vibrate at speed or leak oil on the garage floor.

No wonder the American manufacturers hated them.

Harley-Davidson fought back by promoting its bikes as American-made. To fiercely patriotic Americans, that meant something. To many North Americans, bigger was still better. This included a bigger sound and feel. Just the rumble of the Harley symbolized power.

The rivalry between American and Japanese motorcycle riders continued. It was so intense that when Harley-Davidson released the Fat Boy motorcycle in 1990, it became the subject of an urban myth. Rumor had it that the name was chosen as a deliberate dig at Japanese motorcycle manufacturers; the name was a combination of the nicknames of two of the atomic bombs dropped on Japan during World War II: "Fat Man" and "Little Boy." It was nonsense, of course. Fat Boy had been named because of the width of the machine, which was topped off by a dual gas tank.

Also, the Japanese weren't the only ones making inroads on the North American two-wheeled vehicle market in the 1960s. Harley-Davidson had to overcome a challenge on a second front. Across the Atlantic, the Italians had successfully conquered Britain and were gearing up for an invasion of North America.

A scooter would be leading the charge.

8 MODS VS. ROCKERS– SCOOTERS VS. MOTORCYCLES

One of the most stylin' scooters of all time, known today for its sleek curves and sex appeal, started off as a lame duck.

Donald Duck, to be exact.

When the Piaggio company launched its prototype scooter in 1946, they named it Paparino, the Italian name for the Disney cartoon character.

By the mid-1950s, Vespas were being manufactured around the world. Italy is still the largest market; there, stylish women in skirts and men in designer suits ride Vespas around town.

The company must have hoped the cute name would sell the machine, but customers saw its bulky body as ugly, and only about 500 were sold.

Piaggio's designers went back to the drawing board and produced a second prototype, this one with a step-through body and contoured curves. Company owner Enrico Piaggio took one look and said it looked like a *vespa*, the Italian word for wasp.

The name stuck.

Two decades later, on the beaches of Brighton and other British seaside resort towns, teenage Vespa riders got into fist fights with motorcycle riders over which was better, a scooter or a motorcycle. These "mods" (short for "moderns") were passionate about the scooters they drove, which were as much a fashion accessory as their designer suits and army-surplus parkas. They loaded up their scooters with extra horns, lights and crash bars, long aerials topped with flags or raccoon tails—and so many mirrors their front ends looked like insects bristling with antennae.

To this day, people are either scooter riders or motorcycle riders. In the minds of most people, scooters are "cute." They're for women, or for teens who will eventually graduate to a "real" motorcycle. Yet scooters and motorcycles are essentially the same thing: two-wheeled motorized vehicles. It's funny to think of people getting into fist fights over which is better—after all, you don't see people who drive Volkswagen Beetles duking it out with people who drive Mercedes.

FROM HOPELESS TO HIP

Scooter riders think of their machines as a curvy, elegant form of transportation—about as far from a motorcycle as a three-piece suit is from torn blue jeans. But the earliest scooters looked like toy scooters, the kind a kid stands on and pushes with

This vintage toy kick scooter was the model for the first motor scooters. The brake over the front wheel was a simple foot-activated pedal.

one foot. The only addition was a motor over the front wheel, in the case of the Autoped, or over the back wheel, as on the Motoped, both of which were built in the U.S. in the 1910s. The handle of the Autoped could be folded down so that this "wonder of the motor vehicle world"—as the ads called it—could be tucked away in an office closet after a commute to work.

"LEATHERS"

Protective jacket and pants worn by motorcycle riders.

What's the Difference?

A scooter differs from a motorcycle in both its shape and in the way a rider sits on it. The rider sits upright, as if in a chair, rather than straddling the seat with feet on pegs as a motorcycle rider does. A scooter's engine is hidden inside the body, over the rear wheel, while a motorcycle's engine is at the center of the bike, mounted inside a diamond-shaped, bicycle-style frame.

Scooters are less stable than motorcycles and don't handle as well because they have smaller wheels. Their smaller engines mean they can't go as fast as a motorcycle.

But neither scooter really caught on, even though the famous pilot Amelia Earhart cruised around airfields on a Motoped.

Scooters were also manufactured in Britain. The Skootamota was introduced in 1919, but only survived until 1923, perhaps because even its top speed was too slow for customers. The Autoglider and the Unibus were other British scooters of the 1920s. Unlike scooters of later decades, they weren't big sellers with teens, probably because they were aimed at adult buyers. A Unibus ad shows a businessman in suit, tie, and bowler hat,

sitting "as comfortably as in a chair" as he rolls sedately along on his scooter.

Over in the U.S., scooter builders also marketed their machines to middle-aged commuters and homemakers. The Salisbury Motor Glide of 1936, a model utterly lacking in style, was advertised as "sturdy, safe, economical, comfortable and dependable." The seat was plunked on top of a square body that looked like a metal box on the back end of a bike. Its big selling point, in these lean Depression years, was its incredible gas mileage, while its automatic transmission made it simple to drive. Instead of a throttle and brake, it simply had "stop" and "go" pedals.

American scooters gradually became more curvy and streamlined, evolving into machines with two-tone paint jobs, chrome trim, and intricate vents in the side. Gradually, manufacturers woke up to the fact that teenagers were a potential market, since scooters were cheaper and easier to operate than motorcycles, not to mention an unspoken attraction—their lack of power made parents more agreeable to a purchase.

Ride Anywhere for LESS!

75 MILES PER GALLON

No wonder you see so many Cushmans, everywhere! Thousands ride 'em because they're so Amazingly Economical! Think of getting 75 miles to the gallon! Cheaper than shoe leather! Far less than bus fare and no long waits.

Even more impressive is Cushman's advantage in traffic—its ease of handling, fast get-away, its ability to slip in and out of narrow places. You get there quicker and easier—then, you park anywhere! Wonderful for getting to work, school, market, doing errands, making deliveries. Dependable, safe, comfortable. Powered by famous long-life Cushman "Husky" engine. Powerful quick-acting brakes.

FREE See your Cushman dealer for demonstration of new 1950 models. Or, mail card to Dept. M3

DEALER INQUIRIES INVITED

CUSHMAN MOTOR WORKS, Inc
LINCOLN NEBRASKA USA

Cushman scooters were America's answer to the European models that flooded the market after World War II. "Second car out of the picture?" one late 1940s ad asked. Scooters were cheap solutions for families that couldn't afford two vehicles. Cushman continued to build scooters until 1965.

The Italians, however, were the ones who added style and sex appeal to the scooter—although initially that wasn't their intention. When Vespas and Lambrettas were introduced, Italy was still recovering from World War II. The war had destroyed much of the country's road and train system and led to a rise in fuel prices. The post-war scooter boom was a matter of practicality: a scooter could get Italians where they needed to go.

"ROAD RASH"

Scraped skin from an accident.

Even Harley-Davidson got into the act at the height of the scooter craze. The Topper was produced from 1960 to 1965. It had a pull start, similar to that found on a lawn mower.

Italian scooter makers, however, knew what sold. They set out to redefine the scooter as "sexy." In the 1950s, Vespa put out calendars of beautiful women posing beside their scooters and awarded scooters to the winners of beauty pageants. Movie stars appeared in their ads.

The 1953 Hollywood film *Roman Holiday* helped introduce the Italian-built scooter to North Americans. It also defined the scooter as a vehicle for romance. In it, a young princess, played by Audrey Hepburn, runs away from her duties and has a whirlwind romance with a dashing American reporter, played by Gregory Peck. In one scene she drives unsteadily through the streets of Rome with Peck seated behind her, struggling to help her steer. Chased down and arrested by motorcycle cops, the pair is hauled off to the police station. Peck lies to the police, saying he and Hepburn were on their way to church, by Vespa, to get married. Smitten by this romance, the police drop all charges.

By the late 1950s scooters were the vehicle of choice for British teens who couldn't afford a car. Both the scooter and the motorcycle offered the freedom to escape on weekends to resort towns and hang out with friends, but the scooter was the favorite for the fashion conscious who scorned the typical motorcycle rider's boots and leather jacket as "greasy." They rode Vespas and "Lammys" (Lambrettas)—two-wheeled machines that were stylish enough for their mod look.

The British built scooters, too. The Sunbeam was produced by BSA (Birmingham Small Arms) from 1959 to 1964. "Simple controls," Sunbeam promised. Simplicity was a big selling point for scooters in the 1940s. An American manufacturer called Salisbury carried this philosophy even into its scooter's controls: instead of a "throttle" or "brakes" there were "stop" and "go" pedals on its Model 85.

RIOTS AT BRIGHTON

Just like some modern soccer fans, many of the scooter riders and motorcycle riders of the 1960s loved to fight. The rivalry between them came to a head in the summer of 1964, when mods and rockers faced off at seaside towns in southern Britain. The most famous of the clashes was at Brighton on a bank holiday weekend in May, when up to a thousand teens got into fist fights, smashed bottles, and busted up beach chairs. Both sides threw stones at police. A couple of people were

"TON-UP"

Riding a motorcycle at 100 miles (160 kilometers) per hour or more.

Café Racers and "Ton-Up" Boys

When they weren't trading punches with mods, rockers had other ways to amuse themselves. One of their favorite pursuits was "doing the ton-up."

Ton was slang for 100 miles (160 kilometers) per hour. To do a ton-up was to crank the speedometer into triple digits.

In the 1960s "café racers" tried to outdo each other in illegal races on Britain's motorways. Motorcyclists met at restaurants like the Ace Café in London and raced to the next café. Sometimes they would put a record on and try to complete a circuit of road and return to their starting point again before the song ended. They called themselves "ton-up boys."

The café racing tradition continues to this day. One American-based club, the Ton-Up Pirates, offers commemorative T-shirts and pins to those who receive a traffic citation while moving at triple-digit speed. One recent recipient was a rider who did 105 miles (170 kilometers) per hour in a 15-mile-per-hour (25-kmph) zone. "We hope he gets his license back soon," the club webmaster commented.

Talkin' 'bout my generation... and the next one, and the one after that. Scooters were a hit with the "mods" of the1960s, and today, some scooter clubs continue to perpetuate the same fashions and music.

knifed, several others were injured, and there were dozens of arrests. The tabloid newspapers had a field day.

Mods and rockers were on everyone's mind. In the 1964 Beatles film *A Hard Day's Night*, Ringo Starr is asked if he's a mod or a rocker. His reply: "a mocker."

Mods and rockers were also strictly divided along musical lines. The rockers bopped to the rock 'n' roll of Elvis or Gene Vincent, while mods listened to Motown, a fast-tempo style of reggae called ska, and British bands such as The Who.

By 1966 the conflict was already coming to an end. Mods and rockers were out, hippies were in. Suits and scooters gave way to love beads and Volkswagen vans.

Then came the 1979 film *Quadrophenia*, partially filmed in Brighton, the scene of the 1964 riots. It was based on the concept album of the same name by The Who. It chronicled the downward spiral of an amphetamine-popping mod named Jimmy. Driven to despair by the loss of his girl, his job, and his scooter, he winds up sending a stolen scooter over a cliff.

Despite the downer ending, the film prompted a scooter revival. British mod revival bands like The Lambrettas and the Merton Parkas had a brief heyday in the early 1980s. Even today, members of scooter clubs decorate their scooters with multiple mirrors, put on suits, skinny ties, and parkas, and ride to ska revivals. In Brighton they offer walking tours of the

Vespa G.S.

Italian scooter makers Vespa and Lambretta played up the romance of riding a scooter. In 1962 Vespa came up with the slogan *Paradiso per due* ("Paradise for two"). Ads that featured both a man and a woman on the scooter almost always pictured the man driving, with the woman as a passenger, but a few ads did show women alone on their own scooters. Scooters were popular with women at a time when only men were considered capable of driving a big motorcycle.

paradiso per due

spots where *Quadrophenia* was filmed.

Perhaps the biggest selling point of a scooter was that it was not a motorcycle. In a 1960s ad campaign, Vespa proudly proclaimed, "The difference between a Vespa motorscooter and a motorcycle is that your neighbors won't move out of the neighborhood when you drive home on a Vespa."

The ad pretty much summed it up. Scooter riders care what the neighbors think—bikers don't. Sleek curves or not, a "real" motorcycle rider wouldn't be caught dead on such a lame duck.

Night traffic on the streets of Hanoi, Vietnam.

STOP Jukebox maker David Rockola was one of the first scooter manufacturers to market to young people. In the late 1930s ads for the Rock-Ola scooter showed teens riding and having fun.

MOTORCYCLES HIT THE MAINSTREAM

It's true that the motorcycle was a "biker's" machine in the 1960s. But in the 1970s they hit the mainstream. By the 1980s the typical Harley-Davidson buyer was a man in his 40s with enough money to afford the typical bike's five-digit price tag. Once a cheap form of transportation for the working man, motorcycles were increasingly becoming the playthings of "rubbies" (rich urban bikers). Multimillionaire Malcolm Forbes not only rode a motorcycle but also formed his own club, the Capitalist Tools, whose "colors" consist of preppie-looking red polo shirts. Women were also riding in increasing numbers, a fact that prompted Jo Giovannoni to found, in 1985, *Harley Women*, a magazine for women who rode.

A motorcycle and the wide open road of the Cabot Trail on Cape Breton in Nova Scotia is all this rider needs to feel free.

With so many ordinary people riding motorcycles in the 1980s, it was possible for the movie biker to be a good guy. *Mask* (1985) portrayed bikers as tough guys with a soft spot, willing to protect and comfort a kid with a disfiguring disease. Crazy, violent bikers could only be found in science fiction movies like *Mad Max 2: The Road Warrior* (1981). With many of the real-life

Hells Angels cooling their exhaust pipes in jail, small-town America felt safe from the biker menace. Only in post-apocalyptic wastelands could movie bikers still cut loose and be truly scary and sadistic.

The motorcycle wheeled its way into general cultural acceptance. Stars like singers Tina Turner and Cher posed with motorcycles, and two members of the disco band the Village People dressed up as a biker and traffic cop. The *CHiPs* TV series (named after the acronym of the California Highway Patrol) glamorized motorcycle cops. The show, which ran from 1977 to 1983, stared Erik Estrada and Larry Wilcox—good looking, clean-cut cops who never seemed to get helmet hair. Set in Los Angeles, the series featured lots of car chases along California's scenic highways, multi-vehicle pileups, and disco music. It was a huge hit, tying in with the

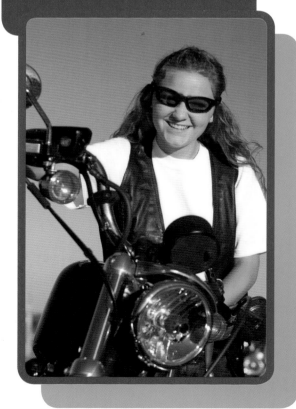

The number of women in motorcycling has grown enormously since the 1960s. Back then, motorcycle gear for women didn't exist. Today, women themselves are manufacturing everything from chaps to choppers.

"BUBBLE GUM MACHINE"

Police Motorcycle.

Happy in Black Leather

Motorcycles have been featured on screen ever since the first silent films. Over the years, they became a fashion statement.

When the TV show *Happy Days* first aired in 1974, the executives at ABC Television had a problem with one of its characters. Fonzie, a young mechanic with greased-back hair and a way with the chicks, looked a little too much like a member of an outlaw motorcycle club for their liking. They insisted he only wear his black leather jacket when riding his motorcycle, and suggested that he wear a nylon windbreaker the rest of the time.

The show's creator, Garry Marshall, pulled a fast one on them. During the show's first two seasons, every scene that involved Fonzie had him sitting on a motorcycle—in his black leather jacket. Years later, that same leather jacket would be inducted into the Smithsonian National Museum of American History.

A hit TV series called *Happy Days* was made in the 1970s but set in the 1950s. The show featured a cool character named Fonzie (left), who always wore a black leather jacket. In this episode, the show's clean-cut star character, Ritchie, tries out Fonzie's bike.

immensely popular TV series *Charlies' Angels* in the ratings during the 1979-1980 season.

THE EVEL ONE

TV was also the place where you could see real-life motorcyclists performing crazy, but entertaining, stunts. Among those motorcycle stunt riders, one name stands out like a superbike among mopeds.

Evel Knievel.

Knievel wasn't the first to launch himself off a ramp over automobiles, nor was he the last. Since his heyday in the 1970s other riders have surpassed him with even more spectacular stunts. Johnny Airtime, for example, rode head-on with a train,

then took off from a jump a split-second before the train smashed into it. But it was Knievel whose name became a household word.

Robert "Evel" Knievel was inspired to go into stunt jumping as a kid after seeing Joey Chitwood's Auto Daredevil Show. He started by jumping his bicycle off ramps made from garage doors and charged the neighborhood kids two cents each to watch. He got his first motorcycle at age 13. In 1965 he formed Evel Knievel's Motorcycle Daredevils, a stunt troupe that rode motorcycles through walls of fire, or jumped over rattlesnakes and mountain lions. In 1966 he turned it into a solo act.

In 1977 Evel Knievel (left) played himself in *Viva Knievel!* and starred alongside model-actress Lauren Hutton (right). The movie used footage of Knievel's real-life jumps—here simulated with multiple images of Knievel for an advertising poster.

FROM BONESHAKERS TO CHOPPERS

Daredevils can be found all over the world. In China, 24-year-old Zhu Chaohui jumped his motorcycle 43 meters (141 feet) across a waterfall on the Yellow River in 1999. In France, Alan Prieur jumped his motorcycle off a mountain top and did a freefall for 154 meters (500 feet) before letting go of his bike and opening a parachute.

A motocross competitor seems to defy gravity as he flies over a jump.

On New Year's Day 1968 Knievel performed a 46-meter (151-foot) jump across the fountains in front of Caesars Palace, a Las Vegas gambling casino. He cleared the fountains, but crash-landed and wound up in a coma for 29 days. Film footage of the jump aired on ABC's *Wide World of Sports*, giving him instant fame.

A series of stadium performances followed. Knievel jumped cars, delivery trucks, double-decker buses, and a tank filled with sharks. He crashed numerous times, suffering, over the years, a total of 37 broken bones. He fractured his skull and sternum, and broke his nose, jaw, upper and lower back, clavicle, ribs, both arms and wrists, hip (it was replaced with a ball and socket), knee, femur, ankles, and toes.

Knievel's most famous jump came in September 1974, when he attempted to leap across Idaho's Snake River Canyon, which is .8 kilometers (one half-mile) wide. He built the rocket-propelled Skycycle specially for the stunt. It failed to clear the gap in test runs, but Knievel went ahead anyway. The Skycycle managed to launch, but its parachute opened

With their sleek curves and colorful paint jobs, modern chopper motorcycles have become works of art. They are a far cry from the "chopped up" bikes of the 1940s that were made with hacksaws.

Easy Rider

Right in the middle of the biker-film craze of the late 1960s, motorcycle movies made a hard left turn when, in 1969, *Easy Rider* cruised onto movie screens across North America.

Part cross-country road trip, part drug trip, *Easy Rider* yanked the handlebars out of the hands of bikers and handed them to hippies. It told the story of two free-wheeling drug dealers who smuggle cocaine into the U.S. from Mexico inside the gas tanks of their ultra-customized choppers.

Although films like *Motorcycle Gang* had touched on the theme of "motorcycle equals freedom," *Easy Rider* drove it home. But freedom had its price. At the end of the movie, the two main characters meet a violent end, blasted off their motorcycles by shotgun-wielding Southern rednecks.

It's about freedom, man. Dig it? Groovy. The 1969 film *Easy Rider* was part cross-country road trip, part drug trip. It showed motorcycles as part of the hippie counter-culture.

immediately. Instead of crossing the canyon, the bike fell into it. Miraculously, Knievel escaped with minor injuries.

Knievel was everywhere. His life story was told in the movies *Evel Knievel* (1971), and *Viva Knievel!* (1977), in which Knievel himself starred. He also appeared as himself on the 1970s TV show *Bionic Woman*. Kids got to know him through the Evel Knievel comic, or the Evel Knievel line of toys that included a stunt cycle, chopper, and super-jet cycle with "spark-shooting jet pods."

Even fictional characters imitated his stunts.

In a 1975 comic, Batman, the "world's greatest crimefighter," teamed up with stunt rider Devil Dayre, the "world's greatest motorcyclist." When Dayre was kidnapped, it was up to Batman to jump the jet-cycle over Torres Canyon.

On a two-part 1975 episode of the TV series *Happy Days*, Fonzie became "Fearless Fonzarelli" and jumped 14 garbage cans with his motorcycle. Like many of Knievel's jumps, the garbage-can leap had a painful conclusion. Fonzie crashed and wound up in hospital with an injured knee.

As late as 1990, TV shows were still making references to Knievel. *The Simpsons* episode "Bart the Daredevil" featured the stunt jumper Captain Lance Murdock leaping a pool filled not just

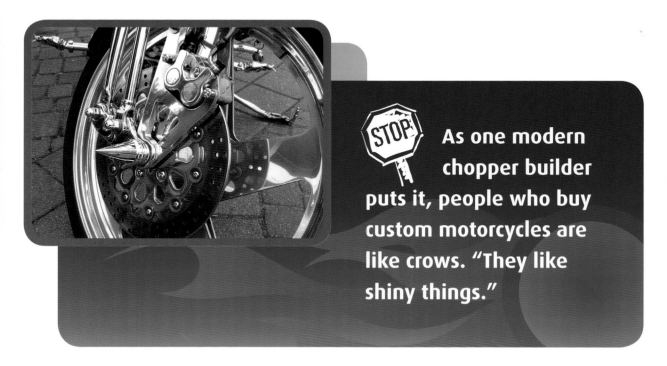

As one modern chopper builder puts it, people who buy custom motorcycles are like crows. "They like shiny things."

"APE HANGERS"

High handlebars that cause the motorcyclist to ride in a position with hands higher than shoulders.

with sharks but electric eels, piranhas, alligators, and a lion. Murdock clears the jump—then trips and falls into the tank. The animals break every bone in his body except for his thumb.

Knievel raised the stunt-riding bar, in terms of both showmanship and originality. Jumpers who followed in his exhaust-filled wake have leaped their bikes over increasingly unusual obstacles, including helicopters with spinning blades. One stunt jumper attached a hang-glider to the top of his bike for some real air time. Another carried his Burmese python along on the jumps. Many of these stunt riders wore white leathers with stars and stripes, patterned after Knievel's trademark suit.

CHOPPED AND BOBBED

Around the time that Evel Knievel was making a name for himself, a style of motorcycle that had been on the fringes was also revving its way into the mainstream: the chopper.

The first choppers were created for practical reasons. Also known as "bobbers," they were racing motorcycles that had been stripped of all excess weight—parts were usually chopped off with a hacksaw—in order to make them faster. Racers stripped off all "unnecessary" extras: fenders, crash bars, windshields, chain guards, mufflers—even brakes.

By the late 1940s outlaw motorcycle clubs had decided they liked the idea of a stripped-down, lightweight, fast machine. Some gave their motorcycles a distinctive look by adding wider-than-stock handlebars, or by replacing the knobs on the end of their shifters with oversized dice.

It wasn't until the 1960s, however, that the true "chopper" was born. Like so many other fads, it started in southern California.

The chopper of the 1960s was a minimalist machine. Headlights were replaced with smaller ones. Foot controls moved forward on the frame, producing a "laid back" riding posture. Front wheels grew skinnier and shed their brakes; rear wheels grew fatter.

The gas tank shrank to a "teardrop" shape, the better to reveal the engine. Everything that could be covered in chrome, was. Some customizers even gold-plated engine parts. Body putty was used to mold over welds and provide a smooth, sculpted look. Seat upholstery was elaborately stitched. Exhaust pipes—without mufflers, and with lots of chrome—grew to elaborate proportions and twisted upwards.

Motorcycle frames, with their flowing curves, now looked like sculptures. Handlebars climbed to the sky—the tallest were known as "ape hangers." "Sissy bars" at the back of the bike also grew.

Chopper builders extended the front forks of their machines, in some cases by crazy amounts. In part, this modification had a practical purpose: "raked" and extended forks handle better under rapid, straight-line acceleration. That was a bonus for long-distance riding on the highways of North America, but not so good for turning.

Police started pulling over chopper riders for safety inspections—especially if they were members of outlaw motorcycle clubs. Riders fought back by doing the bare minimum to comply with regulations. If a law called for a rearview mirror, they attached a tiny dentist's mirror—the regulations hadn't specified how big the mirror had to be.

CHOPPERS FOR EVERYONE

Choppers had appeared in earlier films, but *Easy Rider* (1969) popularized them as nothing had done before. Suddenly everybody wanted one.

After *Easy Rider* was released in Europe, bikers there started emulating what had been a strictly North American fad. The Scandinavians took it to its limit. One impossibly long Swedish bike included forks that were three times as long as the body of the bike itself.

Every part of a bike can be customized for people who want to design their own choppers. Here, even an air filter is given a special style.

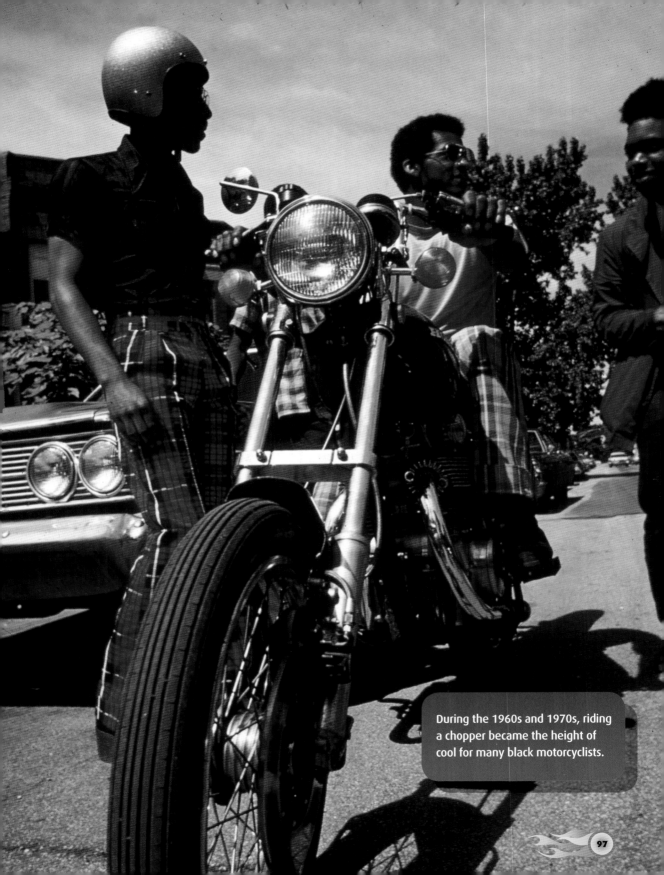

During the 1960s and 1970s, riding a chopper became the height of cool for many black motorcyclists.

Back in North America, toy makers were quick to capitalize on the chopper fad. A number of plastic model kit companies produced chopper bikes and trike models in the 1970s, and a line of Hot Wheels "chopcycles" appeared.

Kids could ride their own "choppers" —bicycles that were styled like custom motorcycles. The Schwinn Sting-Ray bike, released in 1963, was the first. It had high "gooseneck" handlebars, an elongated "banana seat," and a small frame and tires. Later versions had an automobile-style stick shift mounted on the frame—a feature that was discontinued after it was deemed unsafe in 1974.

Advertisements gave chopper-style bicycles a hint of outlaw motorcycle club danger. According to the ads, a kid on a bike with high handlebars and motorcycle-style seat could be "the leader of the pack."

Japanese cosplayers (from "costume players") dress up as bosozoku for the 2004 Comiket—the world's largest comic convention—in Tokyo, Japan.

Even some comic book heroes started riding choppers. Ghost Rider was an amalgamation of demon and man. As the Ghost Rider, stunt motorcyclist Johnny Blaze dressed in a black leather jumpsuit and rode a red motorcycle of "crimson hellfire" powered by "brimstone engines." The demon trapped in his human body gave Blaze a flaming skull head. The imagery is pure biker—the skull and flames can be found on tattoos and rings, and on motorcycle "colors" worn by a host of outlaw motorcycle clubs.

Modern choppers cost tens of thousands of dollars and are rolling works of art. TV shows such as *American Chopper* have turned what was once a homemade hacksaw job into a mainstream consumer product. But although the modern chopper has gone commercial and become very, very expensive, it still remains the ultimate symbol of individualism and personal freedom for many motorcycle riders.

"SISSY BAR"
Bar at the back of a motorcycle, meant to prevent the passenger from sliding off the back.

THE TRIBES OF JAPAN

At the same time that choppers were going mainstream in North America, a unique form of anti-establishment motorcyclist was taking shape across the Pacific. They named their "tribes" after the kamikaze, the suicide pilots of World War II who slammed their aircraft, loaded with explosives, into U.S. ships. They permed their hair, taunted police and drove recklessly on motorcycles with blaring horns and loud exhausts.

STOP At the peak of *bosozoku* activity, in 1980, police estimated that 89 people had died as a result of *shinai boso* (reckless rides), and that more than a thousand had been injured.

They were the *bosozoku*, the "speeding tribe."

In mid-1970s Japan, groups of young people in their late teens and early 20s started taking motorcycles and low-rider cars on *shinai boso*, reckless, high-speed rides through city streets. Using their cars to block intersections and with motorcycles zigzagging across traffic to thwart police pursuit, the tribes vied with each other to be seen and heard. They dragged kickstands along the ground in a shower of sparks. Or they spun their bikes in rubber-burning circles, pivoting around the front wheel, in a "maddo makkasu," a move inspired by the Mad Max films.

Like the outlaw motorcycle clubs of North America, the *bosozoku* proudly displayed their colors—embroidered tribe names on immaculately tailored jackets. No ride was complete without the *htamochi*, the group's flag bearer, sitting on the back of a bike and waving a flag with the tribe's name on it—names like the Fierce Tigers, the Hell Tribe, the Midnight Crazies and the Ostracized. Everything was designed to shock *ippanjin* (ordinary people), from the slogans taken from ultra right-wing organizations or *yakuza* (organized crime) to the "shit squat" crouch—as if squatting over an Asian-style toilet—that tribe members adopted when posing for the press.

"RUBBIES"

Rich urban bikers.

In a move reminiscent of the North American Lynch Report, the Japanese Cabinet issued a 1981 "white paper" that called for the elimination of the *bosozoku*. Penalties for reckless driving were increased, and several local governments banned teenagers from owning motorcycles. Gas-station owners were urged to refuse to sell fuel to anyone riding or driving a modified vehicle, and video-game centers and karaoke parlors were asked to prohibit *bosozoku* from hanging around their establishments.

By police estimates, *bosozoku* activity was cut in half, though the legacy lived on in the comic book *Akira*, and in the 1988 film by the same name.

The motorcycle may have entered the mainstream, but a handful of riders still insisted on going against the grain.

10 GOING TO EXTREMES

Two dirt bikes race neck and neck through an urban wasteland, engines wailing as their riders flail at each other with chains and nail-studded baseball bats. A hill looms ahead. The riders take it, grabbing some huge air. Twisting their handlebars, they throw their bikes sideways or even flip upside down—insane stunts. One straightens out just in time, landing safely—the other crashes and burns.

Kevin Marino of the Starboyz stunt team performs a no-handed wheelie.

Cursing, the player of the video game starts over.

Real-life motorcycle riders may not be duking it out in post-apocalyptic urban wastelands, but they are performing stunts every bit as alarming as those in computer games like *Extreme Biker*. And they're driving the cops nuts.

They call themselves "extreme" street-bike racers. They're the ones who tear through traffic at high speed, pulling a block-long wheelie. Or maybe a head-stand on the bike's gas tank with the throttle locked on. Or a "leap of faith" —a stunt that sees the rider stand on the seat, leap up into the air, and land on his bike again. These daredevils seem hungry for attention-grabbing stunts.

On their websites, they post warnings that their stunts are dangerous—some-thing that should only be attempted by professionals—plus reminders to wear safety gear. But they don't practice what they preach. Instead they perform in jeans, T-shirts, and sneakers. If given helmets,

they disdainfully "bowl" them down the highway. The photos on their websites are brag shots of their injuries, including grue-some close-ups.

They're crazy, no doubt about it. According to some people, they give motorcycling a bad name. But they're also admired. Their motorcycles look

The Starboyz of Akron, Ohio, are stunt riders who push their motorcycles to the limit. Here, Scott Caraboolad drags a subframe.

cool—scuffed up and held together with duct tape and zap straps, the seats covered in brightly colored faux fur. The riders themselves look cool, with their muscles, tattoos, dreadlocks, and bleached Mohawks. And the names of their stunt teams are cooler still: Starboyz, Team X-Treem, Wheelie Boys—and the Miami Warriors, whose ranks include none other than Rob Marley, son of reggae superstar Bob Marley. They're part of the modern "extreme" movement that started in the 1990s with stunts on skateboards, snow-boards, and BMX bikes. That movement today has spawned extreme sports channels, clothing, sports gear, and soft drinks.

It had its roots, however, in the stunts performed by individual motorcycle riders in the 1980s.

"STOPPIE"

Braking suddenly to make the rear wheel of the motorcycle lift off the ground. In a "rolling stoppie," the bike keeps rolling forward on its front wheel.

Doug Domokos was named "the wheelie king" for his ability to perform ultra-slow wheelies in a near-vertical position. He pulled wheelies on top of the Empire State Building in New York, and passed his motorcycle driver's license test on one wheel. His biggest claim to fame

With "extreme" being the flavor of the moment, old-fashioned motorcycle stunts are being ramped up to new limits. The "wall of death," popular in the 1940s, has evolved into the "globe of death"—a sphere made of wire mesh. Motorcycles whip around the inside of this see-through sphere, getting up enough speed to travel upside down across the top. Sometimes up to three riders race around inside the ball at once.

was a single, continuous, 233-kilometer (145-mile) wheelie across the southwestern desert in the U.S. in 1984, a record that remained unbroken for eight years.

British rider Gary Rothwell "skied" behind a motorcycle moving at 250 kilometers (155 miles) per hour, sliding off the back of his bike and holding on. The key to the stunt was his titanium-soled boots, which sent sparks flying out behind him—regular boots would have disintegrated as they ground against the pavement. The stunt was inspired by Dutch rider Artie Nyquist, who skied behind a motorcycle on wooden shoes.

Modern extreme riders have developed a host of tricks that simply weren't possible on earlier motorcycles. In "switchback insane," for example, the rider goes from a backwards-facing handstand into a headstand with arms and legs extended. The "seesaw" is a wheelie-stoppie-wheelie combo.

Extreme riders aren't just daredevils—they're also entertainers, performing at motorcycle shows. Some add extra flourishes like twirling *nunchakus* or breathing fire while performing their stunts. Others attach skid plates to the backs of their bikes that send up sparks when they pull a wheelie. Some write their initials on the pavement by doing a complex, twisting burnout.

Others just try for the biggest air possible. Some are tackling jumps nearly twice as long as Knievel's Caesars Palace jump while twisting their bikes or kicking their feet out to the side while in mid-air.

Motocross riding gives the arms, shoulders and thigh muscles an excellent workout. Riders must control their bikes while speeding over terrain that most people would find difficult to cross on foot.

A new sport known as freestyle motocross (FMX) was developed by those who, in the mid-1990s, started performing BMX freestyle moves on motocross bikes. FMX stunts are dangerous. Broken bones are common, and a rider who lands wrong stands a good chance of winding up brain damaged, in a wheelchair—or in the morgue. Many of the riders have steel pins or scars from past operations.

Picking up on the extreme theme, comic book characters are riding their motorcycles harder than ever before. Batman's sidekick, Robin—now on his

The Opposite of Extreme

Not everyone's into "extreme," of course. Some people aren't into risking their lives on high speed and big air. They just want to get where they're going in one piece.

In 2000, BMW (Bavarian Motor Works) showed off a concept bike it said was the ultimate in motorcycle safety. The BMW C1 featured a "roll cage" that arched over the rider's head, shoulder-high protective bars, and twin seat belts that crossed over the rider's chest. The company claimed the two-wheeled machine was as safe in a head-on collision as a compact car, and that it could be ridden without a helmet.

Riders didn't like it, however. Motorcycle magazines dismissed it as "silly looking." A few thousand C1s were sold in 2001 and 2002, and then BMW ceased production.

BMW tried to lure new riders by releasing this CI motorcycle, which promised the ultimate safe riding experience. Few of the safety models sold, however, and production stopped after 2002.

own and calling himself Nightwing—once used a customized motorcycle to escape a biker gang by leaping his motorcycle from rooftop to rooftop.

Now that's extreme.

THE EVOLUTION OF EXTREME

In the beginning, there was scrambling.

Back in the 1920s, when motorcycle riders wanted to push their machines to the limit, they raced against each other cross country, in what was then known as "scrambling." In the 1940s scrambling evolved into "motocross," which involves racing around a track built on natural terrain including plenty of hills. Motocross competitors take these hills at speed, flying through the air in a series of jumps.

In the 1970s, the sport went indoors to artificial dirt tracks constructed inside

"INSANE"

Doing a handstand on the motorcycle.

stadiums. "Supercross" got its name from the first indoor motocross event, held in 1972 in Los Angeles, which promoters billed as the "Superbowl of motocross."

Drag racing is another sport that tests both motorcycle and rider. Originally, these illegal races would start when the light turned green at an intersection on the "main drag" of town. Today it requires specialized machines and facilities.

STOP In Eastern Europe and Scandinavia, ice racing is a popular sport. Here, motorcycles equipped with steel-spiked tires race around an oval of slick ice. The riders lean sharply into the turns, using kneepads to slide along. They also wear leather masks to prevent flying ice chips from cutting their faces. Their bikes have no brakes—who could hope to stop on ice?

Motocross racers compete on an out-door course filled with tight corners, hills, and bumps that launch them into the air. Racers must complete as many laps as they can during a 10- to 40-minute "moto." The bikes for motocross have a long seat, knobby tires, high clearance and plenty of suspension. They're geared for swift acceleration rather than for extended high speeds.

Modern motorcycle drag racing—held on drag race tracks, rather than public roads—pairs up the fastest machines against each other, and the clock. The bikes are long and low, with a wheelie bar out the back to keep them from flipping over under the force of all that acceleration. The rider lies almost prone on the machine, feet stretched out behind.

Pairs of racers "tack up" their rear wheels for extra traction by spinning them in place until they're sticky and smoking, then advance to the starting line on either a quarter-mile or one-eighth-mile track. When the lights on the "tree" go green, the riders take off, reaching speeds of up to 365 kilometers (227 miles) per hour. Reaction time is everything, since a motorcycle drag race can be won by as little as 1/100th of a second. A race can be over in less than 6.5 seconds.

Like these hard-knock, high-speed races, modern "extreme" motorcycling pushes both motorcycle and rider to their limits. But in the world of extreme, it's not just about winning a race. It's about building the biggest ramp possible and jumping the furthest distance, preferably while performing a crazy stunt. Or it's about thinking up a wild new stunt you can attach your name to.

It's about being famous.

Stayin' Alive

According to some studies, a motorcycle rider is 26 times more likely to be killed in a crash than a car driver who covers the same distance. Most high-speed motorcycle crash victims suffer some sort of serious injury. That's why it's important to wear bright clothing, a helmet certified to be safe, and to enroll in a riding course.

WHAT'S AHEAD?

How do we define a motorcycle today? That depends on where you live. In the Third World, small-engined, two-stroke motorcycles are still what they were to North Americans during the Depression: a practical way to get the family around. In the developed world, however, the motorcycle is primarily a recreational machine. While it is a functional means of transportation for many, the motorcycle taps into our urge to be part of a group. To belong. To be "different together," as one longtime motorcycle rider and author put it.

Some writers compare motorcycle riders to centaurs—half-human, half-horse creatures from Greek mythology—or to modern cyborgs. Whatever the metaphor, the motorcycle has become an extension of the human body, and many riders talk in almost mystical terms about being one with their machines.

Perhaps that's why motorcycles, unlike cars, almost cry out for customization, be it a raked front end, a colorful mural as personal as a tattoo on the gas tank, or the deliberate clutter of a "rat bike" with its abundance of strapped-on gear.

From motorcycling's earliest days, not everyone had the stamina or desire to ride a motorized "boneshaker." Today, many reject a machine that leaves them totally exposed, both to the weather and the risks of the road. But those who jump on the seat of a motorcycle know a joy that others will never experience: the sense of freedom that comes on the open road.

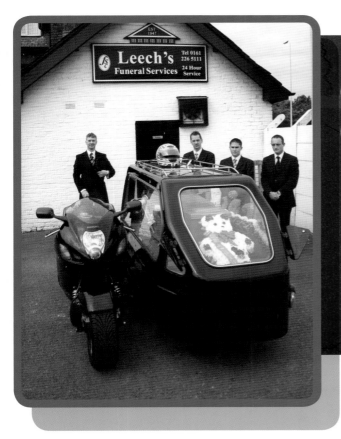

A Life of Motorcycling

For some people, motorcycling is something they do from cradle to grave. Many people get their first taste for motorcycles when playing with toy bikes. In England, Motorcycle Funerals Ltd. offers a "dignified final ride" in a sidecar hearse for those who wouldn't be caught dead in a car.

PARTIAL LIST OF SOURCES

Bachman, Scott, and Sam Cassel, and Tracey Cassel, and Kevin Nelson. *Evel Ways: A Daring Approach to Life*. Minneapolis: GraF X Publishing, 1999.

Barger, Ralph "Sonny." *Hell's Angel: The Life and Times of Sonny Barger and the Hell's Angels Motorcycle Club*. New York: Harper Collins, 2002.

Burns, Max and Ken Messenger. *The Winged Wheel Patch: A History of the Canadian Military Motorcycle and Rider*. St. Catharines: Vanwell Publishing, 1993.

Dregni, Eric and Michael Dregni. *Scooters!*. Osceola: Motorbooks International, 1995.

Ferrar, Ann. *Hear Me Roar: Women, Motorcycles and the Rapture of the Road*. New York: Crown Publishers, 1996.

Ganneau, Didier and Francois-Marie Dumas. *A Century of Japanese Motorcycles*. Osceola: Motorbooks International, 2001.

Lovell, Buck. *American Police Motorcycles: A Photo History of Police Motorcycles*. Stillwater: Wolfgang Publications, 2002.

Seate, Mike. *Choppers*. Osceola: Motorbooks International, 2003.

Seate, Mike. *Street Bike Extreme*. Osceola: Motorbooks International, 2002.

Seate, Mike. *Two Wheels on Two Reels: A History of Biker Movies*. Conway: Whitehorse Press, 2001.

Sucher, Harry V. *The Iron Redskin*. Newbury Park: Haynes Publications, 1977.

Thompson, Hunter S. *Hell's Angels: A Strange and Terrible Saga*. New York: Ballantine Books, 1966.

Wagner, Herbert. *At the Creation: Myth, Reality and the Origin of the Harley-Davidson Motorcycle 1901-1909*. Madison: Wisconsin Historical Society Press, 2003.

Walker, Alastair. *Scooterama*. Osceola: Motorbooks International, 1999.

Wright, Stephen. *American Racer 1910-1940*. Huntington Beach: Megden Publishing Co., 1979.

FURTHER READING

Books

Dregni, Michael. *The Spirit of the Motorcycle: The Legends, the Riders, and the Beauty of the Beast.* Stillwater: Voyageur Press, 2000.

Walker, Mick. *History of Motorcycles.* London: Hamyln, 2000.

Wilson, Hugo and Dave King. *Ultimate Motorcycle Book.* New York: DK Publishing, 1993.

Wilson, Hugo. *Ultimate Harley-Davidson.* New York: DK Publishing, 2003.

Websites

Harley-Davidson Motorcycles (www.harley-davidson.com)

Indian Motorcycles (wgby.org/localprograms/indian/)

Motorcycle Hall of Fame Museum (www.motorcyclemuseum.org)

Pioneers of American Motorcycle Racing (www.statnekov.com/motorcycles/)

Motorcycle City:The Bikes of War (www.motorcyclecity.com/military-motorcycles.htm)

Welbike (www.alliedspecialforces.org/soewelbike.htm)

American Motorcyclist Association (www.ama-cycle.org)

United Sidecar Association (www.sidecar.com/Files/SC%20Manual.pdf)

Women's International Motorcycle Association (www.inzani.demon.co.uk/history.html)

Honda (world.honda.com/history)

Kawasaki (www.khi.co.jp/mcycle/museum/index_e.html)

Yamaha (www.yamaha-motor.com/sport/company/historyhome/home.aspx)

Vespa (www.vespausa.com/company/history.cfm)

Cushman scooters (www.nebraskahistory.org/sites/mnh/cushman2.htm)

Evel Knievel (www.stevemandich.com/evelincarnate)

Motorcycle Stunt Jumpers (www.geocities.com/cyclejumper_2000)

AMA Motocross (www.amamotocross.com)

White Helmets (www.army.mod.uk/royalsignals/whelmets)

Guggenheim Museum: The Art of the Motorcycle (www.guggenheim.org/exhibitions/past_exhibitions/motorcycle)

Bell Helmets (www.bellbikehelmets.com/timeline.asp)

Batman's Batcycle (www.1966batmobile.com/batcycle1.htm)

PHOTO CREDITS

cover © Irvin Cheung; i: (top) istockphoto.com/Kyle Maass; ii: Photo by David "foto" Avila. Photos courtesy Starboyz; iv: © istockphoto.com/Sue McDonald; 2: © istockphoto.com/George Ihring; 3: used with permission of *Popular Science Magazine*; 4 (top), 55, 69, 86, 91, 108, 112: © iStockphoto.com; 4 (bottom): © iStockphoto.com/Lara Seregni; 5: courtesy National Motorcycle Museum in Amamosa, Iowa; 6: courtesy Science & Society Picture Library, London, England; 7: photo courtesy Phoenix Museum of History and Dave Kimball; 8: © iStockphoto.com/Maciej Feodorów; i, 10, 16, 22, 26, 27, 30, 33, 39, 43, 50, 52: courtesy Tom Samuelsen, Pacific Northwest Museum of Motorcycling; 11: courtesy Motorcycle Hall of Fame Museum Collection; 12: courtesy Rick Howard and Stephen Wright; 13, 14, 19 (bottom), 21, 24, 25, 34, 35, 46, 47, 49 (left), 54, 59, 81: courtesy Harley-Davidson USA; 17: courtesy Yonkers Police Historical Society; 19 (top): Douglas Motorcycles; 23: courtesy Glenn H. Curtiss Museum, Hammondsport, NY; 29: courtesy Craig Dove; 32: courtesy Irbit MotorWorks of America Inc.; 36: Kavanaugh's War Postals; 37: courtesy B.C. Dragoons Collection, Okanagan Military Museum BCD-P-867-1-1; 38: courtesy Bundesarchiv at Koblenz (Bild 101-725-184-22); 40: courtesy Imperial War Museum, H30628; 41: used with permission Harley-Davidson USA; 44, 48: City of Vancouver Archives photo CVA 99-2794; 49 (right): courtesy National Archives and Records Administration. Photograph No. 532256 "Santa Clara County, California. Motorcycle and Hill Climb Recreation...." 04/05/1940; Records of the National Youth Administration, 1934 – 1945; Study of Youth Photographs, 1940, Record Group 119; National Archives at College Park, College Park, MD; 53: courtesy Motorcycle Hall of Fame Museum Collection; 56: courtesy American Motorcyclist Association; 58, 65, 89, 90, 93: © courtesy Kobal Collection; 60: © CPJournal de Québec/Benoit Gariepy; 62: © Dick Willis, reprinted with permission; 64: American Fore Insurance Group ; 68: Joseph Buegeleisen Co. ; 70: courtesy Gloria Huyck; 71: used with permission of Honda; 72: courtesy National Archives and Records Administration. Photograph No. 547857; "Young New Yorker Ready to Roar off on his Honda" June 1973; Records of the Environmental Protection Agency, 1944 - 1999; DOCUMERICA: The Environmental Protection Agency's Program to Photographically Document Subjects of Environmental Concern, 1972 - 1977, Record Group 412; National Archives at College Park, College Park, MD; 73: used with permission Universal Music Enterprises; 74: © iStockphoto.com/Andrea Leone; 77: © iStockphoto.com/Raimond Siebesma; 78: © iStockphoto.com/Earle Provin; 79: © iStockphoto.com/David Asche; 80: used with permission of Cushman: a Textron company; 82: used with permission of BSA Regal; 84: © Detour Records, UK, courtesy David ("Dizzy") Holmes; 85: courtesy Piaggio Foundation and Museum; 87: © iStockphoto.com/David Elfstrom; 88, 109 (top): © iStockphoto.com/Danny Bailey; 92: © iStockphoto.com/Alan Goulet; 94: © iStockphoto.com/Wayne Stadler; 96: © iStockphoto.com/Rob Simmons; 97: courtesy National Archives and Records Administration. Photograph No. 556206; "Black Residents of Chicago's West Side Check Out a Motorcycle...." June 1973; Records of the Environmental Protection Agency, 1944 - 1999; DOCUMERICA: The Environmental Protection Agency's Program to Photographically Document Subjects of Environmental Concern, 1972 - 1977, Record Group 412; National Archives at College Park, College Park, MD; 98: courtesy of stormstill (www.flickr.com/photos/stormstill); 101, 102: © David "Foto" Avila, courtesy Starboyz; 104: © iStockphoto.com/Rob Zeiler; 105: courtesy Bavarian Motor Works (BMW); 107: © iStockphoto.com/Lynette Schauwecker; 109 (bottom): © iStockphoto.com/Kyle Maass; 110: © iStockphoto.com/Jay Spooner; 111: © Rev. Paul Sinclair, courtesy Motorcycle Funerals, UK.

ACKNOWLEDGMENTS

Thanks to the following people for their assistance with the research that went into this book:

Craig Dove, great-grandson of Effie Hotchkiss, for providing a copy of *Wheels in My Head*, her memoir.

Patrick Dowling of the Whatcom Museum of History & Art (www.whatcommuseum.org).

Pete Gagan of the Antique Motorcycle Club of America (www.antiquemotorcycle.org).

Jo Giovannoni of Open Road Radio (www.openroadradio.com), co-founder of *Harley Women* magazine.

Bevan Jones of the Trev Deeley Motorcycle Museum (www.trevdeeley.com/custom/collection.html).

Dave Kimball of Lewiston, New York, for information on Lucius Copeland.

Allan "Zippy" Lowson of the Laughing Indian Riders motorcycle club.

Thomas (Tom) Samuelsen of the Pacific Northwest Motorcycle Museum (www.pnwmom.org).

Bob Vickers of the Greater Vancouver Motorcycle Club (www.gvmc.ca).

ABOUT THE AUTHOR

Lisa Smedman is the author of numerous science fiction and fantasy novels, including *Extinction*, which made the *New York Times* bestseller list for hardcover fiction. She is an avid gamer and is a co-founder of *Adventure Unlimited*, a roleplaying magazine. She also works as a journalist for a community newspaper.

As a teenager Lisa enjoyed many long-distance trips riding pillion on friends' motorcycles. Later she bought her own bike: a 50cc machine. She currently lives in British Columbia and travels on four wheels.